# CHURCH
# REFORMED

# CHURCH
# REFORMED

TIM BAYLY

*Church Reformed*

Warhorn Media
2401 S Endwright Rd.
Bloomington, IN 47403
WarhornMedia.com

Unless otherwise indicated, all Scripture quotations are from the NEW AMERICAN
STANDARD BIBLE®, © 1960, 1962, 1963, 1968, 1971, 1972, 1973, 1975, 1977, 1995 by
The Lockman Foundation. Used by permission.

Cover design by Ben Crum
Interior layout by Alex McNeilly. Typeset in 11/14 Garamond Premier Pro.

Printed in the United States of America
23   22   21   20   19        1   2   3   4   5

ISBN-13: 978-1-940017-21-1 (paperback)
ISBN-13: 978-1-940017-22-8 (EPUB)
ISBN-13: 978-1-940017-23-5 (Kindle)

*To Mary Lee*

# Contents

# Foreword

**T**IM AND I HAD A PROFESSOR IN SEMINARY who urged his students not to write a book before we were forty. I took his meaning to be that a book written too soon would be written out of pride, untested theories, and ivory-tower notions. Don't try to teach someone to walk before you've learned how to walk with a limp. Books about the church written before forty would be without the seasoning and maturity that come from hours in living rooms, in garages, in counseling sessions, in funeral homes, in long elders meetings, in the trenches.

Tim passed forty years a good while ago (sorry to remind you, old friend). He is now into his fourth decade of pastoral ministry. During the first decade, Tim and I pastored an hour and a half from each other in the same denomination. About once a month we packed up our families after morning worship and took turns spending our Mondays in each other's homes. The conversations always turned to our churches, to the needs of the sheep, the personal crises, the challenging pastoral situations. There was never an end to the needs and opportunities to seek and give counsel. Iron sharpened iron.

While changes in churches added distance, the phone calls and emails hardly slowed down. Over the years I watched Tim grow sharper in mind and softer in heart, stronger in biblical conviction and clearer in counsel. In a word: wise.

Tim's wisdom and experience is applicable across the Church today because his wisdom and experience have been gained from across the Church. He has served in rural churches, small-town churches (you can't get much more "small town" than Pardeeville, Wisconsin—trust me, I've been there), and university-town churches. He has spent as much time in barns and fields as he has in coffee shops and well-appointed offices.

Of the writing of many books there is no end, and this certainly applies to books on the Church. They tell us church should be simple, deliberate, visioneering, counter-cultural, emerging, purpose-driven, attractional. Books wring their hands over why people don't go to church or are leaving the church.

The solutions they offer are superficial, often pragmatic and consumeristic, designed to entertain and meet the felt needs of the goats rather than lead and spiritually nurture the sheep. Too many books are written by hirelings rather than by real shepherds.

This book is different. The messenger is different and the message is different.

This book is written in the spirit of the apostles. In the spirit of Peter exhorting elders to shepherd the flock of God, exercising oversight, willingly as God would have you (1 Peter 5:2). In the spirit of Paul who pleaded with the Ephesian overseers to shepherd and defend the flock from fierce wolves attacking the church from inside and out, drawing the sheep away. In the spirit of the senior apostle, John, loving and exhorting and warning so the church may keep herself from idols and not sin.

Tim takes to heart the warning of Hebrews 13:17, that leaders will give an account for the souls under their care.

He loves the Church with a fatherly love, with tenderness and firmness, with grace and truth in generous doses, with warnings, admonition, and wisdom. And when his words cut, it's the wound of a friend. If you don't want your conscience pricked, then don't read this book.

But if you walk away, just know there are precious few voices in the

Church today willing to say what Tim has to say. He is a much needed gift to the body of Christ, a necessary gift. When have you heard writers of books on the Church today say, "He who will not have the church as his mother, cannot have God as his Father"?

This is the work of a true father of the faith who has loved his flock as his own children, and they know it. There is no theory here, no untested hypotheses. This is wisdom gained from living it out. This is iron sharpening iron.

Tim loves the Church. How do I know?

Well, first of all, I have worshiped in all the churches Tim has served. I can testify to the love shared between the flocks and their shepherd. I have seen the fellowship, the intimacy, the love and care for one another. I have been a bit jealous of the genuine sense of community.

Second, I have seen Tim confront sin. And is that not the greatest sign of love? Is that not like the love of God toward us, that He disciplines those He loves and chastens us as sons?

Third, because Tim has given his life's energy to defending pure doctrine and the purity of Christ's body. This has cost him in so many ways, yet he has been unwavering for truth and for purity.

Peter tells husbands to live with their wives in an understanding way. This book is about living with, and in, the Bride of Christ in an understanding way. In a way that will lead her to become more holy, cleansed with the washing of water with the word.

Of course any book on the church worth its salt is going to address the seminal and foundational text on the church, Acts 2:42. But hold on to your hat, because Tim is not going to say all the usual things many say about it that lack understanding.

He urges us to recommit ourselves to be devoted to the apostles' teaching, to fellowship, to the breaking of bread, and to prayer. This is a call to return to real intimacy, real authority, real love.

This is a book about heaven on earth, to borrow the title of the last chapter. What grace and blessing that God should call us out of the world and give this precious gift, a foretaste and glimpse of heaven here on earth. We are to love what He loves and honor what He honors. Our labor for her is not in vain.

Do you love the church? Do you love the Bride of Christ? Do you love the Body as much as you love the Head? Do you love the sheep? What is the proof, the evidence?

Satan has been assailing Christ's Church from the very beginning, and his relentless assault will never cease until Christ returns. So into the midst of this battle, Christ's faithful followers must be equipped. This is a book about helping us love the precious, blood-bought body of our Lord Jesus Christ the way He does.

A young pastor reading this book will be helped to start on the right course and avoid many pitfalls in ministry.

The older pastor reading this book will be helped to see the way toward finishing well.

For all the "called-out ones" in the pew, this book is a wonderful sword, making one fit to wage war with boldness and courage in this postmodern world that hates authority and truth.

Someone told Augustine to take up and read. I say, take up and drink. This book is a hearty red wine, well-aged with wisdom, filled with the aroma of Christ.

*Soli Deo Gloria.*

Robert Woodyard
Senior Pastor
First Christian Reformed Church
Lynden, Washington

# *Acknowledgments*

**F**IRST, MY DEAR MARY LEE: SHE HAS LISTENED to this book many times over the course of a decade, giving helpful feedback and providing significant editing—a delightful first for us.

Second, my eldest son Joseph: for his careful thinking and wise counsel.

Third, my brother David: he did a thorough edit, saving me from many mistakes.

Fourth, Pastors Stephen Baker, David Curell, Jody Killingsworth, Alex McNeilly, Jacob Mentzel, Phillip Moyer, and Lucas Weeks: as I worked, they patiently listened and gave encouragement.

Fifth, the session of Trinity Reformed Church: finally, they told me to get the book done, Or Else. Not wanting Else, I got it done.

Sixth, Andrew Dionne: he provided critical help in the chapter on prayer.

Last, Nathan Alberson, Jacob Mentzel, and Alex McNeilly: in the end, the brunt of the work getting this text into useful form fell on them. No author has better editors.

# CHURCH
# REFORMED

*Be on guard for yourselves and for all the flock, among which the Holy Spirit has made you overseers, to shepherd the church of God which He purchased with His own blood.*

*—Acts 20:28*

# First Things

AROUND MY HOMETOWN OF BLOOMINGTON, INDIANA, you'll occasionally see a bumper sticker with a picture of a steepled church and the words "Love Your Mother."

The bumper sticker was inspired by a conference on the Church[1] we held several years ago. A young mother in our congregation designed it.

Christians love the Church. Paul writes in Ephesians that the Church is the Bride of Christ. Jesus loves the Church and gave Himself up for her. What He loves we must love. How could it be otherwise for those redeemed by His blood?

But sadly, today it *is* otherwise among many who claim to love Jesus.

Recently I visited a man who is dying. A lifelong student of Scripture, he knows the Bible inside out, yet he has forsaken the assembly of believ-

---

1. I've done my best to use an uppercase *C* in contexts referring to the universal Church, and a lowercase *c* in contexts referring to particular or local churches. The distinction is not always very clear.

ers. Each Lord's Day he sits at home while his wife joins God's people in worship. This wasn't the first time I visited a man close to death who knows God's Word but refuses to worship with the people of God in a local church. Another man I knew dropped his wife off for worship each Sunday yet refused to enter himself.

How can a man love Jesus and not love His Bride?

Jesus commands us to love one another, yet how are we to understand "one another" if we repudiate and condemn our fellow Christians? How can we obey if we will not join ourselves to Christ's Church?

Of course we all admit the difficulty of loving the Church. Isn't that the point?

When I was young, my mother had an annoying habit of spitting on her Kleenex to clean food off my face.

Sometimes it's hard to love your mother, yet God commands us to honor our father and mother. What honor does a mother deserve more than love? She carried us in her womb for nine months. She bathed, nursed, clothed, loved, kissed, taught, and disciplined us. What love!

So it is with the Church. She cares for God's children in the same ways our earthly mothers care for us. Scripture names her "mother"[2] and we are to love her.

But sadly, during the second half of the twentieth century, Western Christians left their Mother behind.

## Leaving the Church Behind

In October 1985 my father began his twenty-fifth (and final) year as a columnist for a periodical for evangelicals called *Eternity*. His column that month was titled "The End of an Era" and summarized what his generation of evangelical leaders had received as a legacy and what they were leaving to their children.

---

2. See Galatians 4:26. In his comments on Isaiah 54:13, John Calvin says, "Isaiah . . . gives the appellation of 'children of the Church' to those who are 'taught by the Lord.' If they are her children, they must then have been conceived in her womb and nourished by her, first 'with milk, and next with solid food,' as Paul says (1 Corinthians 3:2), till they 'grow up and arrive at manhood (Ephesians 4:13).'" *Commentary on the Book of the Prophet Isaiah*, trans. William Pringle, Calvin's Commentaries (Calvin Translation Society; Baker Books, 2003), 2:146–47.

Here are a few excerpts:

We inherited three or four small independent seminaries; we bequeath nine or ten healthy institutions that are the major source of trained evangelical leadership for America's churches and parachurch movements.

We inherited one national youth movement—Christian Endeavor, working through the local church.... Parachurch youth organizations we founded include Youth for Christ, Young Life, InterVarsity Christian Fellowship, and Campus Crusade for Christ.

... we inherited denominational, church-centered programs for children, youth, and adults. We bequeath Child Evangelism Fellowship, Christian Service Brigade, Pioneer Ministries, Christian Business Men's Committee, Bible Study Fellowship, Neighborhood Bible Studies, Christian Medical Society, Christian Legal Society, Nurses' Christian Fellowship, and many other parachurch programs....

We inherited Christians who were loyal to the church.... We bequeath Christians who are loyal to many religious organizations in addition to—sometimes in preference to—their church...[3]

Through much of the twentieth century, evangelical Protestantism was the dominant religious force in North America. But, as my father noted, evangelicals did not commit their lives to building the Church. Rather, they poured their talents into founding parachurch missions, colleges, seminaries, youth ministries, camps, evangelistic crusades, radio stations, publishers, professional associations, and campus ministries.

Evangelicalism's best and brightest did their work outside the church, and though they assumed this work fulfilled the Great Commission, no one stopped to ask why the church no longer mattered.

One of the legacies Evangelicalism has bequeathed to Christians today is a growing separation between becoming a Christian and becoming a member of the Church of Jesus Christ. Our evangelism has called men and women to trust God for the forgiveness of their sins and establish a

3. Joe Bayly, "The End of an Era," Out of My Mind, *Eternity*, October 1985, reprinted in *A Voice in the Wilderness* (Victor, 2000), 224–25.

personal relationship with Jesus. Then we encourage new believers to find a way to continue to grow.

Somehow, though, the Church is no longer viewed as essential to Christian growth. Conferences are great. Facebook groups, music, podcasts, broadcast sermons, discipleship material, Christian books . . . these fruits of evangelical ministry have supplanted Christ's Bride, the Church.

And yet . . . where's "one another" in listening to Christian radio, for example? If we don't like the things the guy says, we just turn him off.

You can't do that in your church's small group. The same guy is rude to his wife week after week. The same woman belittles her husband. In worship the same teenagers roll their eyes when the pastor warns against sexual sin.

This is the Church. These sinful people are our "one another" and we learn to love and forgive them just as they love and forgive us. At least that's how it's supposed to be.

And yet . . . we're tempted to think that—if hearing the Gospel and believing is what Christianity is all about—people come to faith more easily if they don't have to deal with all the drama of the Church: infighting, hypocrisy, abuse of authority . . .

Many young, hip churches, having been schooled by the parachurch, now base themselves on a parachurch model, leaving behind the authority, accountability, and deep relationships among members that lie at the heart of Christ's "one another."

Some Christian men and women are becoming uneasy at this.

They wonder why their church is different from the New Testament church. What's happened to the authority of pastors and elders? What's happened to the authority of Scripture? Why is there so little prayer in our worship? Why don't we read the Bible? Why are there no warnings before we take the Lord's Supper?

Who's keeping watch over my soul? Who's watching over the souls of my children? Why doesn't my pastor know me? Why doesn't the pastor call me to repent? Why does our pastor seem indifferent to couples living together?

God's people are noticing that churches no longer discipline anyone. They are growing uneasy about churches with no authority, no commands, no warnings, no admonitions, no membership, and therefore no excommunication.

No fear of God.

## A Call to Return

This book is a call to return to our Mother and love her. Our love for Christ's Bride should take precedence even over our love for our own families. Our children should know that the elders' discipline of them is our discipline of them. From infancy, our sons should be convinced that their father and mother's first love is Jesus and His body of believers.

The saying is, "Blood is thicker than water," but it's not. Rather, water— the water of baptism—is thicker than blood.

When Christ is our first love, His Bride will come before all of our earthly loves, including the love of husband for wife, father for son, mother for daughter, sister for brother, brother for sister. This is precisely what Jesus means when He warns,

> If anyone comes to Me, and does not hate his own father and mother and wife and children and brothers and sisters, yes, and even his own life, he cannot be My disciple.[4]

And,

> "Who is My mother and who are My brothers?" And stretching out His hand toward His disciples, He said, "Behold My mother and My brothers! For whoever does the will of My Father who is in heaven, he is My brother and sister and mother."[5]

If you've been a Christian for any length of time, likely you've listened to several wedding sermons in which pastors have used Christ's love for the Church to exhort husbands and wives to love one another. But how

4. Luke 14:26.
5. Matthew 12:48–50.

often have our pastors used Christ's love for the Church to command us to love the Church?

> Husbands, love your wives, just as Christ also loved the church and gave Himself up for her, so that He might sanctify her, having cleansed her by the washing of water with the word, that He might present to Himself the church in all her glory, having no spot or wrinkle or any such thing; but that she would be holy and blameless.[6]

Jesus is tender toward His Bride. He loves her. He gives Himself up for her. He sanctifies her. He presents her to Himself in all her glory, with no spot or wrinkle, but holy and blameless.

When Saul was on the road to Damascus intending to persecute the Church, Jesus knocked him to the ground and blinded him. Don't miss the wording of His rebuke:

> Saul, Saul, why are you persecuting Me?[7]

See that word "Me"? Like any husband who loves his wife, when Saul attacked His Bride, Jesus took it personally. An attack on the Church is an attack on Him. Why are we quick to affirm our love for Jesus, yet balk when someone calls us to love His Church?

You may respond that Jesus is perfect and the Church is anything but. Though this is true, the Church's failures and sins are no reason to love her less. They haven't caused Jesus to love her less. He just gets to work. Didn't He say it was the sinners He came for—not the righteous?

Jesus loves the Church, and we should too.

Out of this confrontation on the road to Damascus, Saul, the persecutor of Christ's Bride, was born again by the Spirit of God. He spent the rest of his life proving his love for the Church by suffering for her. And he didn't resent his suffering. He didn't write a book titled *Churches That Abuse*; rather, he considered suffering for Christ's Bride a privilege:

6. Ephesians 5:25–27.
7. Acts 9:4.

Now I rejoice in my sufferings for your sake, and in my flesh I do my share on behalf of His body, which is the church.[8]

We don't love the Church because she's lovable (although she is, and we will come to this later). We love the Church because Jesus loved and gave Himself up for her.

Following His resurrection, our Lord showed the inseparable connection between love for Him and love for His Church. Peter, who had denied Jesus three times the night before Jesus died, was fishing with six other disciples when Jesus showed up and cooked them breakfast.

After eating, Jesus turned to Peter and asked,

"Simon, son of John, do you love Me more than these?"
He said to Him, "Yes, Lord; You know that I love You."
He said to him, "Tend My lambs."
He said to him again a second time, "Simon, son of John, do you love Me?"
He said to Him, "Yes, Lord; You know that I love You."
He said to him, "Shepherd My sheep."
He said to him the third time, "Simon, son of John, do you love Me?"
Peter was grieved because He said to him the third time, "Do you love Me?" And he said to Him, "Lord, You know all things; You know that I love You."
Jesus said to him, "Tend My sheep."[9]

Jesus loves His sheep. He expects His servants to love them also. How can we claim to love Jesus while turning our noses up at the smell of His Flock?

If you have trouble loving the Church; if a church has failed you in the past and you refuse to love and give yourself to the Church now; if you talk contemptuously about "the institutional church"; if you refuse to become a church member; if you say you won't join any church because you submit

8. Colossians 1:24.
9. John 21:15–17.

to Jesus alone; if you attend a megachurch where you're neither known nor loved; if you attend a church where the pastor gives a lecture and knows no more about you than your dental hygienist does; then don't lie to yourself. You don't love the Church any more than a wife who, hurt by her husband, spends the rest of her life refusing intimacy with him.

When we turn from intimacy with the Church, we must realize our Lord Himself has not done so. Will you repent and begin to give yourself to the Church?

When I was a child, one of the most obvious things to us children was Mud[10] and Dad's love for the Church. For more than twenty years Dad taught our local church's main adult Sunday school class, and his teaching was no performance; he probed his class members with tough questions about the Bible passage. He had little patience for *pro forma* answers. The affection of class members for one another was obvious. Members sang, shared (sometimes heartbreaking) prayer requests, and hung around afterwards talking with Mud and Dad and one another.

Mud and Dad often closed the church down Sunday mornings after worship, talking and helping bear the burdens of others on the steps outside the church building long after the senior pastor had gone home for dinner.

Our home was open. Missionaries, pastors, writers, parachurch leaders, children alienated from parents, older singles from our church—all were welcome in our home and at our table. Hospitality is love in action and we grew up helping by setting the table, clearing the table, washing the dishes, and cleaning the kitchen afterwards while the adults talked.

Mud and Dad were supportive of their pastors. When we lived in Philadelphia, our pastor had a heart attack and Dad filled in without pay, preaching and providing pastoral care until he was cleared to return. Mud and Dad were listening ears and wise counselors to their longtime pastor and his wife in Wheaton, encouraging and comforting them in the midst of their hurts and disappointments.

My wife Mary Lee and I have tried to carry on this love for the Church we saw demonstrated in our childhood homes. Has it been a one-way street, we give and the Church takes?

---

10. Our family's affectionate name for Mother.

Absolutely not. All our lives the Church has loved, admonished, rebuked, and comforted us and our children. She continues to do so to this day. When we are gone from our congregation, we miss her. And when we return, we hear again and again that she missed us. Sure, our congregation gets along fine without us, but living in love together, we are missed.

As I said, today many Christians long for a return to real intimacy and authority within the Church. A return to real love and one-another-ing.

But what does this look like? What is the connection between faith, salvation, and the Church? What is the relationship of the Christian to the Church? How does a Christian become a member of the Church? Why should a Christian become a member of the Church?

What is the Church? Who is the Church? What are the sacraments and are they important? What does the Church do, and why?

*She is our mother.*

—*Galatians 4:26*

# CHAPTER I

# *Who Is the Church?*

**T**HE WORD "CHURCH" IS AN ENGLISH TRANS-
lation of the Greek word *ekklēsia*. The New Testament uses this
word over a hundred times and its meaning in Greek isn't at all religious. When the apostles wrote *ekklēsia*, it wasn't a word making people
think of a building where people observed private religious rites.

In Greek, *ekklēsia* is a noun made by compressing the preposition *ek*
(meaning "out") with the verb *kaleō* (meaning "call"). So whenever you
read the word "church" in the New Testament, it refers to "called-out ones."

Keep this meaning in mind, because Sunday morning when Dad says,
"It's time to go to church," he usually means the building where the family
goes each Sunday morning to sing, pray, and listen to the preacher.

But even if we know enough to say the church is not the steeple but the
people, the question remains . . . Which people? And if the answer is the
"called-out" people, then who called them out and from where?

The Bible tells us God called them, and He called them out from the
world. The Church is the body of people God has called out from among
the masses of worldlings who live for this world and do not know Him.

## The Bible's Called-Out Ones

Writing to the church in Rome, the Apostle Paul speaks of "our father Abraham."[1] He calls Abraham the Church's father because God called Abraham out too. God said to Abraham, "Go forth from your country, and from your relatives and from your father's house, to the land which I will show you."[2]

All through Scripture we have accounts of God calling His people out from the world. In fact, we might describe Scripture as the history of God calling His people to Himself.

God called Enoch and he walked with God straight into Heaven. God called Noah to leave his neighbors and enter the ark. God called Lot out of Sodom. God called the children of Israel out of Egypt.

When Jesus was preaching, He called the crowds to Himself: "Come to Me, all who are weary and heavy-laden, and I will give you rest."[3] At the very beginning of his letter to the church in Rome, the Apostle Paul tells them, "you also are the called of Jesus Christ."[4]

The Church is the people God calls out from the world and sets apart to holiness. The Church is the people God loves.

## The Bride and the Body

Let me clarify something important. Although the Church is made up of those who are called out of the world by God, none of those individuals is the Church. Scripture names the Church the "bride" of Christ.[5] Individual Christians are not the Bride of Christ. Christ's Bride comprises all those He has called out from the world, and it's only together that they become Christ's Bride, the Church.

Jesus gave Himself up for His Bride. This is the glory of membership in His Church. Together we are His beloved Bride:

1. Romans 4:12.
2. Genesis 12:1.
3. Matthew 11:28.
4. Romans 12:6.
5. Revelation 19:7; 21:9.

Christ also loved the church and gave Himself up for her, that He might sanctify her, having cleansed her by the washing of water with the word, that He might present to Himself the church in all her glory, having no spot or wrinkle or any such thing; but that she should be holy and blameless.[6]

Jesus presents the Church—not individuals—to Himself as His holy and blameless Bride.

I'm not denying that Jesus loves individual members of the Church and gave Himself up for them. But He redeemed them individually from their sins to incorporate them in His Bride. Because Jesus gave Himself up for the Church, no individual ever has safety outside the Church. Thus, from the very first centuries the Church has never stopped warning individuals that those who refuse to have the Church as their mother cannot have God as their Father.[7]

Outside the Church there is ordinarily no hope of salvation. This has been the teaching of the Church across two millennia.

The Protestant Reformers were clear on this. Martin Luther writes,

Therefore he who would find Christ must first find the Church. How should we know where Christ and his faith were, if we did not know where his believers are? And he who would know anything of Christ must not trust himself nor build a bridge to heaven by his own reason; but he must go to the Church, attend and ask her.

Now the Church is not wood and stone, but the company of believing people; one must hold to them, and see how they believe, live and teach; they surely have Christ in their midst. For outside of the Christian church there is no truth, no Christ, no salvation.[8]

John Calvin expresses this same truth with characteristic tenderness:

6. Ephesians 5:25–27.
7. See Cyprian, *On the Unity of the Church* 6.
8. Martin Luther, "Second Christmas Day," sermon, accessed March 7, 2019, http://www.godrules .net/library/luther/129luther_a6.htm.

But because it is now our intention to discuss the visible church, let us learn even from the simple title "mother" how useful, indeed how necessary, it is that we should know her. For there is no other way to enter into life unless this mother conceive us in her womb, give us birth, nourish us at her breast, and lastly, unless she keep us under her care and guidance until, putting off mortal flesh, we become like the angels. Our weakness does not allow us to be dismissed from her school until we have been pupils all our lives. Furthermore, away from her bosom one cannot hope for any forgiveness of sins or any salvation. . . . God's fatherly favor and the especial witness of spiritual life are limited to his flock, so that it is always disastrous to leave the church.[9]

Pastors from many different church backgrounds who wrote the Westminster Confession of Faith took this truth for granted, declaring,

The visible Church . . . is the Kingdom of the Lord Jesus Christ, the house and family of God, out of which there is no ordinary possibility of salvation.[10]

In their Belgic Confession, the Reformed churches of Europe's Low Countries declare the same:

We believe that since this holy assembly and congregation is the gathering of those who are saved and there is no salvation apart from it, no one ought to withdraw from it, content to be by himself, regardless of his status or condition.

But all people are obliged to join and unite with it . . ."[11]

So . . . Do we demonstrate the same love and submission to the Church we show our own mothers? Does the thought of losing her scare us to

9. John Calvin, *Institutes of the Christian Religion*, trans. Ford Lewis Battles, 4.1.4.

10. Westminster Confession of Faith, 25.2, accessed March 7, 2019, https://reformed.org/documents/wcf_with_proofs/index.html.

11. "The Obligations of Church Members," Belgic Confession, art. 28, accessed March 7, 2019, https://reformed.org/documents/BelgicConfession.html.

death? Do we humble ourselves to speak of being her "pupil"?

We must admit that few of us think of the Church this way. We do not ascribe such importance to her.

Rather, our view of the Church is like our view of a personal trainer. Disciplined, healthy people don't need one, but if you're lazy it may be helpful to have a time and place where you place yourself under external pressure to huff and puff—an appointment where you'll be missed if you don't show up.

Most of us think we don't need the Church in order to have "a personal relationship with Jesus." Still, we're quick to admit it strengthens us to spend a little time each weekend with other people who love Jesus like we do. It gives us a spiritual vibe.

This is not what Scripture says about our relationship to the Church. God calls us out from the world and places every last one of us at the bosom of His Bride to be nursed and cleaned and instructed and disciplined until we put off this mortal flesh.

Scripture declares, "Now you are Christ's body, and individually members of it."[12]

That word "you" is not singular. It's plural. Maybe you've never thought carefully about the meaning of these words for your thinking and posture toward the Church, but you'd be wise to do so: "The body is one and yet has many members, and all the members of the body, though they are many, are one body."[13]

It's only as we are joined to the one Body of Christ that we have life. We are not the Body of Christ individually. No one of us is the Church. The Church is all those for whom Christ died.

Alone, every man is picked off by Satan and devoured. To have our Great Shepherd's protection, we must stay near Him in His sheepfold, the Church. Alone we are helpless. So says Proverbs—over and over:

> There is a way which seems right to a man,
> But its end is the way of death.[14]

---

12. 1 Corinthians 12:27.
13. 1 Corinthians 12:12.
14. Proverbs 16:25.

There is a kind who is pure in his own eyes,
Yet is not washed from his filthiness.[15]


When one sheep goes out from the sheepfold, he is "lost." So says Jesus. Yet He goes on to reassure us the good shepherd goes out and searches for that lost one to bring him back to the sheepfold.

God has called us out from the world and made the Church our Mother.

15. Proverbs 30:12.

*So then, those who had received his word were baptized; and that day there were added about three thousand souls.*

*—Acts 2:41*

# CHAPTER 2

# Baptism: How We Enter the Church

**F**ROM THE FIRST PREACHING OF THE GOSPEL on the Day of Pentecost, the New Testament records the apostles' work fulfilling the Great Commission by planting churches.

It all started in Jerusalem. At the conclusion of the Apostle Peter's sermon, we read the people were "pierced to the heart" and cried out, "Brethren, what shall we do?"

Peter responded, "Be saved from this perverse generation!"

What step did they take?

Those who had received his word were baptized; and that day there were added about three thousand souls.[1]

Note carefully: those who believed were "baptized" and "added" to the Church.

---

1. Acts 2:37–41.

## The New Testament Pattern

The sacrament of baptism is the first step a new believer takes in obedience to his Savior, and by that step he is united to the Church. We see it in our Lord's Great Commission:

> Go therefore and make disciples of all the nations, baptizing them in the name of the Father and the Son and the Holy Spirit.[2]

We see it with the Ethiopian eunuch:

> As they went along the road they came to some water; and the eunuch said, "Look! Water! What prevents me from being baptized?"
> And Philip said, "If you believe with all your heart, you may."
> And he answered and said, "I believe that Jesus Christ is the Son of God." And he ordered the chariot to stop; and they both went down into the water, Philip as well as the eunuch, and he baptized him.[3]

We see it with Lydia and her household:

> A woman named Lydia, from the city of Thyatira, a seller of purple fabrics, a worshiper of God, was listening; and the Lord opened her heart to respond to the things spoken by Paul. And when she and her household had been baptized . . .[4]

Jesus commanded the apostles to make disciples, "baptizing them in the name of the Father and the Son and the Holy Spirit," and they obeyed.

Skipping to the present, in his book *The Great Good Thing*, Jewish convert Andrew Klavan tells this story about his own baptism. He had come to faith and was praying:

> *Thank you God. I don't know how to respond to this abundance. You have*

2. Matthew 28:19.
3. Acts 8:36–38.
4. Acts 16:14–15.

*given me so much. You've given me everything I wanted since I was a child. Presence of mind and love and a voice and meaning and beauty. You've just handed them to me, gifts, like on Christmas. I don't know how to repay you. I don't know how to begin. You're God and I'm nothing. I can't think of a single thing I can offer you that would matter to you. If there's something I'm missing, tell me. Please. Tell me what you want me to do.*

He goes on to say:

The answer came back to me on the instant, so clear in my heart it might have been spoken out loud: *Now you should be baptized.*[5]

Really, no one needs any special revelation from on high. Scripture records both Jesus' command and the apostles' consistent obedience to that command to initiate souls into His Church through baptism.

Those who had received his word were baptized; and that day there were added about three thousand souls.

Men and women believed the Gospel, were baptized, and that very day were added to the Church. Being joined to the Church through baptism, those three thousand souls gave themselves to the four devotions of the Church—the teaching of the apostles, fellowship, the breaking of bread, and prayer.[6]

### Our Present Disorder

After two thousand years of this order, the Church is falling into disorder. Men and women who have never been baptized nevertheless commune with the family of God around the Lord's Table, claiming for themselves every benefit of God's covenant household. Yet they have never been granted entry to that household by the elders of the Church.

5. Andrew Klavan, *The Great Good Thing: A Secular Jew Comes to Faith in Christ* (Nelson Books, 2016), 242–43.
6. Acts 2:42.

You ask, *What gives the elders the right to say who can and can't come to the table?* And, *Why should elders have authority over baptism and the Lord's Supper?*

Note in the biblical examples above that baptism was not self-administered, nor was it administered by family members. In the New Testament and ever since, baptism into Christ's Church has been administered by church officers. These officers are called elders, pastors, deacons, or bishops, but only officers of Christ's Church should baptize souls into the Church and administer the family meal at the Lord's Table.

Christ had chosen the apostles to lead His sheep and guard His sheepfold, and they in turn appointed elders over the church in each city.[7]

It is the duty of these officers to protect the Church from those who try to enter without going through the door of Jesus Christ:

> Truly, truly, I say to you, I am the door of the sheep. All who came before Me are thieves and robbers, but the sheep did not hear them. I am the door; if anyone enters through Me, he will be saved, and will go in and out and find pasture.[8]

In the Book of Acts, only those who believed on Jesus were granted baptism. And only those who believe on Jesus should be baptized into the Church today. Following the biblical order further, only those united to the Church through baptism by the Church's officers should be allowed by those officers to eat and drink at the Lord's Table.

Our Lord Jesus gave the administration of His sacraments to the officers of His Church—His undershepherds—and it is the obligation of those officers to guard baptism and the Lord's Supper from being profaned by notorious sinners, hypocrites, and worldlings.

Some time ago, elders of our congregation reported to their fellow elders that the young children of one of our more mature Christian couples were taking the Lord's Supper without having been baptized. The parents did not believe in infant baptism and were waiting to have their children

---

7. Acts 14:23.
8. John 10:7–9.

baptized until they made a profession of faith. Meanwhile, their children were taking the sacrament of the Lord's Supper.

This is so common that now, when I administer the Lord's Table, I'm careful to warn those who have never been baptized that they must be united to the household of faith by baptism before they may eat at the family table.

Because of this warning, we have lost some from our congregation and many visitors have been angered. After all, in most congregations no one will restrain them from giving the bread and wine to their unbaptized children.

Yet baptism is a sacrament, and sacraments make human submission to divine authority—and the blessing God pours out on such submission—visible. That's the beauty of sacraments.

### The Old Testament Pattern

In both Old and New Testaments, God commanded His people to observe an external, physical rite of entry to His covenant community. In the Old Testament, the entry rite was circumcision. When God established His covenant with Abraham and his descendants, He instructed Abraham,

> This is My covenant, which you shall keep, between Me and you and your descendants after you: every male among you shall be circumcised. And you shall be circumcised in the flesh of your foreskin, and it shall be the sign of the covenant between Me and you. And every male among you who is eight days old shall be circumcised throughout your generations. . . . But an uncircumcised male who is not circumcised in the flesh of his foreskin, that person shall be cut off from his people; he has broken My covenant.[9]

Entry into the Old Covenant required circumcision and those not circumcised were "cut off." Whether servants or sons, even though they were members of Abraham's household, without circumcision they were cut off from the people of God.

---

9. Genesis 17:10–12, 14.

## Both Circumcision and Baptism
## Are Matters of the Heart

Of course, true faith is not born of baptism. The sacraments are always administered on the basis of prior faith, whether that faith is the faith of the individual or (in the case of infant baptism) his parents.

In the Old Testament, Abraham was justified prior to circumcision, but God commanded that those not circumcised be expelled from His people. God Himself says "no" to those seeking entry to His family without circumcision. He commands that the uncircumcised man "shall be cut off from his people," because "he has broken My covenant."

Now, at this point some people claim a radical separation between the Old and New Covenants. They admit the necessity of circumcision in the Old Covenant, but claim this was because God created the Old Covenant to be a covenant of flesh, whereas with the New Covenant it is now a matter of the spirit and heart. In the Old Covenant, flesh and physical marks, sacrifices, and land were the way of salvation, but in the New Covenant it's all spiritual. They conclude that baptism as a physical rite actually isn't that important.

This is wrong—in both directions.

First, it's wrong in making the Old Covenant a matter of flesh rather than spirit and heart. Second, it's wrong in making the New Covenant a matter of spirit and heart rather than flesh.

While it's true that the Old and New Covenants differ in a number of ways, they don't differ here. Both Old and New Covenants are founded on faith in God and both command a physical rite of initiation by which those who live by faith are marked and welcomed into God's covenant household, the Church.

## God's Covenant Household

Many texts in Scripture demonstrate that circumcision was a matter of the heart. Speaking of the way Abraham, our father in faith, was saved, the Apostle Paul warns against the false doctrine that the work in the flesh of circumcision saved him.

Not at all:

> He received the sign of circumcision, a seal of the righteousness of the
> faith which he had while uncircumcised, so that he might be the father
> of all who believe without being circumcised, that righteousness might
> be credited to them, and the father of circumcision to those who not
> only are of the circumcision, but who also follow in the steps of the faith
> of our father Abraham which he had while uncircumcised.[10]

It's clear: circumcision was a physical seal of the righteousness of spiritual faith which Abraham had before he was circumcised. So in both the
Old and New Covenants, God alone gives the gift of faith which is the
instrument by which a man is transferred from death to life. Faith is not
claimed by any human act. It is a gift of God.

Thus circumcision saved no one and baptism saves no one—the baptism
of the flesh, that is; the washing of water.[11] Marks of the flesh never save
anyone. What God seeks is the heart. The naked sign without the presence
of the thing signified angers Him.

Consider this command given through the prophet Jeremiah:

> Circumcise yourselves to the LORD
> And remove the foreskins of your heart,
> Men of Judah and inhabitants of Jerusalem,
> Or else My wrath will go forth like fire
> And burn with none to quench it,
> Because of the evil of your deeds.[12]

Jeremiah was addressing men who had been circumcised in their bodies,
yet whose hearts were far from God. Thus the circumcision of their bodies
brought on them the wrath of God. A man is justified by faith, alone—
never by works of the Law such as circumcision:

---

10. Romans 4:11–12.
11. See 1 Peter 3:21.
12. Jeremiah 4:4.

For we maintain that a man is justified by faith apart from works of the Law.[13]

Still, pleased to stoop to our weakness, God has bound saving faith to these physical signs. As in the Old Testament, today God is still pleased to mark members of His household with a physical sign by which we are set apart, by which we are distinguished from those who are not members of His household.

In the New Covenant God has given us two physical signs at the heart of our life together as Christians, and we neglect them to our peril.

*What? Our peril? If God has my heart, what difference does it make whether I'm baptized?*

The difference it makes is that God commanded us to be marked with baptism as the sign and seal[14] of our entry into His covenant family.

That's all we need to know—and obey.

If we claim to have faith but rebel against that faith's first fruits everywhere recorded in Scripture, what good is our faith? Make no mistake: the man who trusts in Jesus Christ for the forgiveness of his sins but refuses to submit to officers of Christ's Church by receiving baptism from them under their authority is a rebel against God. He may be rebelling out of ignorance, but the rebellion of ignorance is, nonetheless, rebellion.

Faith alone saves, but true faith is never alone. True faith is always accompanied by obedience, and this obedience starts with the obedience of baptism.

Again, there are things that have changed from the Old to the New Covenants. In the Old Covenant, only males were circumcised, whereas in the New both males and females are baptized. Also, the physical mark itself is different.

Yet baptism and the Lord's Supper are more similar than dissimilar to their Old Covenant counterparts of circumcision and the Passover meal. Both demonstrate continuity rather than discontinuity with their Old Testament parallels—starting with both being commanded by God.

13. Romans 3:28.
14. Romans 4:11.

## What about Infant Baptism?

Now at this point, some of our Protestant brothers might object, claiming that a further difference between the initiation rites of the two Covenants is that the rite of the New Covenant, baptism, is only to be given to those who themselves believe, and not to their children.

Look through church history and it's apparent this is a longstanding debate with men of great godliness and knowledge of Scripture on both sides. Augustine, Martin Luther, and John Calvin are on one side while John Bunyan, Charles Spurgeon, and Martyn Lloyd-Jones are on the other. Can we solve the debate here?

No. It's enough to note the difference and to call every man to study Scripture with the fathers of the Church in order to come to a conviction concerning truth in this matter, recognizing that both sides are agreed that baptism is the necessary path of entry into Christ's Church.

## No Baptism, No Church

Putting aside the matter of whether or not children born to believing parents should be baptized in their infancy, what all must agree on is that baptism is commanded by God, and that membership in Christ's Church and eating and drinking at our Lord's Table must follow it.

Here is the biblical pattern:

- First, a man is given faith in the life, death, and resurrection of Jesus Christ.
- Second, that man obeys His Lord Jesus and requests that the officers of the Church bring him into the Church through baptism.
- Third, through his baptism, that man enters the Church and is welcomed to the family table where we eat and drink in remembrance of our Lord Jesus.

This is not complicated. So why have we turned away from baptism?

## When Reforming the Church Becomes
## Deforming the Church

The answer is that we make a habit of throwing the baby out with the bathwater.

Some years back I had taken a call to a new church and, soon after beginning there, I had noticed there were some in the church who were coming to the Lord's Table without having been baptized. At the time I'd never heard of such a thing and I couldn't figure out how it had started. So I began teaching the congregation that baptism is God's command and must precede communion.

After a few months, at our invitation the founding pastor returned for a visit. A kind man, he agreed to spend some time with me, and that Saturday afternoon we spent several hours talking in our living room. He was a faithful shepherd, a man of great heart who had loved his sheep, and he had good advice for me in many areas.

On one matter, though, I saw I'd have to take a different direction.

Near the end of our conversation, I mentioned that I'd noticed a lack of conviction concerning the biblical basis of baptism among the people of the church, and I wondered why.

He responded by pointing out how common the belief in baptismal regeneration was in the area, particularly among Protestants of the Christian Church denomination so predominant in our part of the country. In order to oppose that error, he said he had avoided putting much emphasis on baptism in his teaching and preaching ministry.

This is common today. Upon coming to faith in Jesus, many who have grown up in churches which teach that the act of baptism removes sin react by neglecting baptism entirely.

This is no way to reform the Church.

The improper use of a thing doesn't invalidate its proper use.

It's no reform to deform the Church. It's no reform to stop obeying biblical commands in order to protect ourselves from unbiblical practices. In Scripture, God has given us everything we need to live a godly life in Christ Jesus and we must follow the pattern of church life the Bible reveals.

## Membership

So what happens after baptism?

If we look at the wording used on the Day of Pentecost, we see that the response of those who believed was, first, that they were baptized; then second, they were "added" to the Jerusalem church:

> So then, those who had received his word were baptized; and that day there were added about three thousand souls.

"There were added . . ." We might pass over this seemingly insignificant phrase, but in this day when men want more than anything else to be autonomous individuals under no authority, we must not miss it. The modern American church has moved away from church membership, but read it again: every one of those baptized was "added" to the Jerusalem church. It was a great day when 3,000 souls joined the home church of the Christian faith there in Jerusalem.

The apostles didn't baptize these new believers into some ethereal entity known as "Christendom." They weren't marked as new members of some wholly spiritual and non-intrusive mystical body known as "the church universal" or "the church invisible."

Rather, they were baptized and became family members of the Jerusalem church. They each became subject to that church's officers. They sat under their leaders' (apostolic) preaching and lived in loving organic fellowship with their brothers and sisters in Christ. They broke bread together at the Lord's Table and gave themselves to prayer. Each person baptized was "added to their number," and from that time on held membership in that specific household of faith which was the Church of the Living God.[15]

Taken as a fabric, initiation into and life within the church of Jerusalem was the direct fulfillment of the Great Commission given this church's apostles by Jesus right before He ascended into Heaven:

---

15. 1 Timothy 3:15.

Go therefore and make disciples of all the nations, baptizing them in
the name of the Father and the Son and the Holy Spirit, teaching them
to observe all that I commanded you.[16]

Fulfilling the Great Commission through the church was about as flesh-
and-blood as anything can be. It involved time and food and money and sin
and righteousness and submission and forgiveness. It was as real as our own
families are, only this was the family of God with every brother and sister
a member by adoption, washed by the blood of Jesus Christ, and baptized
into that family. Yes, a spiritual family, but one with an exceedingly earthly,
fleshly, organic life.

Today in the household of God, we must recover authority and submission to authority, and the most certain path to recovery is reinstituting the
practice of the sacraments laid down for us in the New Testament. This is
the practice we see in the first church in Jerusalem. This is the practice we
see across the Apostolic Age. This is the practice restored to the Church five
centuries ago by the Genevan Reformers. This is the practice which has been
honored by five centuries of Protestant Christians since the Reformation.

The Great Commission is only fulfilled when souls are baptized into
Christ's Church and remain there being fed and cleaned and admonished
and instructed until the day they receive their promotion into the presence
of the Lord.

16. Matthew 28:19–20.

*They were continually devoting themselves to the apostles' teaching and to fellowship, to the breaking of bread and to prayer.*

—*Acts 2:42*

# PART 2

# WHAT DOES *the* CHURCH DO?

**SCRIPTURE RECORDS THAT THE FIRST CHURCH IN** Jerusalem gave herself to four devotions. These devotions were the foundation of the Church.

When we hear the word "devotions," we think individually. We think of our own relationship with Jesus through personal prayer, personal Bible reading, and personal meditation—things we do by ourselves.

Western culture is all about the individual doing things for himself, but God calls us into the Church and we are to embrace what she does for us.

What is it she does for us?

For the first believers on the Day of Pentecost, life together centered on four corporate disciplines:

> They were continually devoting themselves to the apostles' teaching and to fellowship, to the breaking of bread and to prayer.[1]

1. Acts 2:42.

What was the fruit of these disciplines? The historical account continues:

> And all those who had believed were together and had all things in common; and they began selling their property and possessions and were sharing them with all, as anyone might have need. Day by day continuing with one mind in the temple, and breaking bread from house to house, they were taking their meals together with gladness and sincerity of heart, praising God and having favor with all the people. And the Lord was adding to their number day by day those who were being saved.[2]

The church committed to Scripture is built on these four devotions. Now then, let's examine these disciplines so we may have the same priorities as the apostolic church. In order, these devotions are:

1. the teaching of the apostles
2. fellowship
3. the breaking of bread
4. prayer

These devotions are the heart of the Church.

---

2. Acts 2:44–47.

*And every day, in the temple and from house to house, they kept right on teaching and preaching Jesus as the Christ.*

*—Acts 5:42*

# CHAPTER 3

# The Teaching of the Apostles

**T**HE FIRST OF THE FOUR DEVOTIONS OF THE Jerusalem church was the teaching of the apostles.

What did the apostles teach?

We don't need to guess. By God's grace we have a record inspired by the Holy Spirit laid down for us in the New Testament. We must never forget that the words of Christ's apostles are the words of God Himself. First, our Lord Himself taught the apostles before sending them out as His ambassadors. But the Holy Spirit also inspired every word of the New Testament written by the apostles:

> But know this first of all, that no prophecy of Scripture is a matter of one's own interpretation, for no prophecy was ever made by an act of human will, but men moved by the Holy Spirit spoke from God.[1]

The great theologian B. B. Warfield put it bluntly: "What Scripture

---

1. 2 Peter 1:20–21.

says, God says."[2] For this reason the Apostle Peter warns us we would "do well to pay attention [to Scripture] as to a lamp shining in a dark place."[3]

## Apostolic Preaching

In a day when individualism owns our hearts, we need to recognize that the normal tool God has promised to use to call souls out from the world, giving them faith and repentance, is preaching:

> For "Whoever will call on the name of the Lord will saved."
>     How then will they call on Him in whom they have not believed? How will they believe in Him whom they have not heard? And how will they hear without a preacher? How will they preach unless they are sent? Just as it is written, "How beautiful are the feet of those who bring good news of good things!"[4]

We continue to devote ourselves to the teaching of the apostles today by heeding God's Word preached. Those who are "diligent" in their search for God[5] will attend the preaching of the Word each Lord's Day among God's people assembled for worship. Those who hunger and thirst after righteousness will be there, and they'll be attentive.

On the other hand, the unteachable proud man who refuses to eat out of another man's hand will not be there. Or, if his body is present, his mind and heart will be far away.

We cannot devote ourselves to the teaching of the apostles if we neglect the assembly of believers or attend that assembly with pride ruling our minds and hearts. We cannot devote ourselves to the teaching of the apostles if we are resistant to being fed the bread of life by a sinner like us with feet of clay.

God could have chosen another way. He could have used angels, yet it pleased Him to use sinful men. So says the Reformer John Calvin:

---

2. B. B. Warfield, "The Biblical Idea of Inspiration," *The Inspiration and Authority of the Bible* (Presbyterian and Reformed, 1979), 145. See also "'It Says:' 'Scripture Says:' 'God Says,'" ibid., 299ff.
3. 2 Peter 1:19.
4. Romans 10:13–15.
5. Hebrews 11:6 (King James Version).

He could indeed do it ... by the angels; but there are many reasons why he prefers to do it by means of men.

... this is the best and most useful exercise in humility, when he accustoms us to obey his Word, even though it be preached through men like us and sometimes even by those of lower worth than we. ...

Further, nothing fosters mutual love more fittingly than for men to be bound together with this bond: one is appointed pastor to teach the rest, and those bidden to be pupils receive the common teaching from one mouth.[6]

"Nothing fosters mutual love more fittingly" than God's people being fed by a man who is their inferior. Our love for God, for His Church, and for the men He has called to preach to us are inseparably bound together by God's own decree. As our Lord Himself said concerning the preaching office,

The one who listens to you listens to Me, and the one who rejects you rejects Me; and he who rejects Me rejects the One who sent Me.[7]

So although we have the teaching of the apostles recorded in the pages of the New Testament, devotion to their teaching is not simply devotion to a printed Bible—even reading through the Bible each year. Rather, devotion to the apostles' teaching is devotion to the Word of God publicly proclaimed within the assembly by a man called by God to that work. This fallen man has been set apart by the laying on of hands and prayer to fulfill the office of pastor.

He is God's shepherd and God has called him to feed His sheep the pure milk of the Word.

Central to this duty God has placed on him is the fulfilling of his call by leading God's people in worship each Lord's Day:

6. Calvin, *Institutes* 4.3.1. From the same section: "If he spoke from heaven, it would not be surprising if his sacred oracles were to be reverently received without delay by the ears and minds of all. For who would not dread the presence of his power? Who would not be stricken down at the sight of such great majesty? Who would not be confounded at such boundless splendor? But when a puny man risen from the dust speaks in God's name, at this point we best evidence our piety and obedience toward God if we show ourselves teachable toward his minister, although he excels us in nothing..."

7. Luke 10:16; cf. Calvin, *Institutes* 4.3.3.

"But the word of the Lord endures forever."

And this is the word which was preached to you.

Therefore, . . . like newborn babies, long for the pure milk of the word, so that by it you may grow in respect to salvation.[8]

Churches today follow the Jerusalem church's devotion to the teaching of the apostles by gathering to listen to Scripture publicly proclaimed by a man God has set apart to that work in a particular congregation.

## Preaching Is the Center of Worship

Some Christians would deny that preaching is the center of Christian worship. Instead, they'd point to the "Lord's Supper," "Eucharist," or "Mass," declaring this sacrament more important than preaching.

If you have ever attended Roman Catholic worship, you have noticed that the preaching at such services is almost non-existent. The priest talks briefly, quickly moving on to the liturgy and paraphernalia of sacrifice that is the center of the Roman Mass. This is why they refer to attending worship as "going to Mass."

Sadly, an increasing number of Protestant and Reformed pastors today are following Rome's lead in subordinating preaching to the Lord's Supper. Some even brag about how short their sermons have gotten since they changed their church's worship and liturgy to make the Eucharist the center of their worship.

The hard-fought battle of the Reformers against Rome's sacramentalism[9] was not simply a battle over how many sacraments there are—with Rome multiplying them to seven and the Reformers returning to the simplicity of the New Testament's two, baptism and the Lord's Supper. The Reformers also fought Rome's sacramentalism by insisting that the Word and the

---

8. 1 Peter 1:25–2:2.

9. The word "sacramentalism" is being used here to refer to an unbiblical emphasis on signs, symbols, and ceremonies with the promise, whether implied or explicitly stated, that these things communicate saving grace in and of themselves. The Latin phrase *ex opere operato* ("from the work worked") is often used as a shorthand summary of this heresy.

faith only it can produce are essential to all worship, including the Lord's Supper, thereby returning preaching to the preeminent position it held in the Apostolic Age.

## The Synagogue

Even a simple examination of the worship of the New Testament and Early Church is sufficient to show that from the beginning Christian worship reproduced the worship Jesus and the apostles took part in at the Jewish synagogues they faithfully attended.

Where did Jesus preach and teach?

> Jesus was going through all the cities and villages, teaching in their synagogues and proclaiming the gospel of the kingdom . . .[10]

> He came to His hometown and began teaching them in their synagogue . . .[11]

Some would point out that the New Testament church also was devoted to the Lord's Supper and that this was the place where our Lord ordained that Christian worship would differ from the worship of the synagogue.

True, but we must not turn away from the reform of worship bequeathed to us by the Reformers who restored the reading and preaching of God's Word to the center of Christian worship as it had been from the beginning.

It would be good if every church allotted sufficient time for weekly communion. Yet even where weekly communion is practiced, it ought to be evident to all that the Word of God read and preached is the heart of worship as it was in the apostolic church. As one pastor puts it:

> It can be said without fear of contradiction that Christian worship from the earliest times has been characterized by the fact that the Word of God is central. Doctrine is the very soul of the Church.[12]

10. Matthew 9:35.
11. Matthew 13:54.
12. Robert Rayburn, *O Come Let Us Worship* (Baker Book House, 1980), 89.

In his classic work on the history of doctrine, William Cunningham points out how much of the Roman Catholic Church's decline during the Middle Ages was due to its overemphasis on the sacraments:

> It was mainly by the spread of erroneous and extravagant notions upon the subject of the Sacraments, that the fundamental doctrines of the gospel were set aside and perverted.[13]

Historian John Leith writes that one characteristic of the Reformers' liturgy is "the emphasis on hearing and receiving in faith the word of God in word and sacrament. The centrality of the sermon cannot be disputed."[14] James Nichols has similarly pointed out that "the Reformation was a great preaching revival, probably the greatest in the history of the Christian church."[15]

We must weigh the various elements of worship looking for the centrality of the Word of God read and preached. This is the first test of a church's devotion to the teaching of the apostles.

The "teaching of the apostles" is listed first in the four devotions of the Jerusalem church. Commenting on this position in Scripture's listing of these devotions, Calvin says that Luke "begins with doctrine, which is the soul of the Church."[16]

Preaching is the center of the Church's worship, but even when preaching is the center of worship, we must evaluate the preaching to see if its content and delivery communicate the authority of God and the truth of His Word.

---

13. William Cunningham, *Historical Theology: A Review of the Principal Doctrinal Discussions in the Christian Church Since the Apostolic Age*, 3rd ed. (T & T Clark, 1870), 1:202.

14. John Leith, *An Introduction to the Reformed Tradition: A Way of Being the Christian Community* (Westminster John Knox Press, 1981), 184.

15. James Hastings Nichols, *Corporate Worship in the Reformed Tradition* (Westminster Press, 1968), 29.

16. John Calvin, comments on Acts 2:42, *The Acts of the Apostles, Vol. 1 (1–13)*, trans. John W. Fraser and W. J. G. McDonald, ed. David W. Torrance and Thomas F. Torrance (Eerdmans, 1965), 85.

## Authority in Content

They went into Capernaum; and immediately on the Sabbath He entered the synagogue and began to teach. They were amazed at His teaching; for He was teaching them as one having authority, and not as the scribes.[17]

Nearly every time Christians seek to proclaim God's truth today, we are told to shut up. The world is firmly convinced there is no such thing as truth. There are only opinions and feelings, and no one should disagree with someone's opinions because it might make that person feel bad.

This denial of truth flows from the modern man's view of God. He laughs at any god who claims to be over all and in all—any God in whom "we live, and move, and have our being."[18]

The modern man says "my god" without the slightest fear that his god doesn't get along well with anyone else's god. We each have our own personal deity and everyone is careful to speak of their god in a reasonable manner.

It was the same in ancient Canaan, Rome, and Athens. It's called "idolatry," and from Genesis to Revelation Scripture condemns this false form of worship:

> For all the gods of the peoples are idols,
> But the LORD made the heavens.[19]

The violence of the collision between God's Word and man's idols (and the lies he uses to prop them up) is due to no flaw in the Word. God intended it. God decreed such conflict.

God glories in demonstrating the foolishness of man's wisdom. This means those who seek to preach His Word faithfully will face terrible opposition—starting in their own congregation. The only way to avoid it will be to preach hints and suggestions, or a good thought for the week. The only way to avoid it is to preach without authority.

17. Mark 1:21–22.
18. Acts 17:28 (King James Version).
19. 1 Chronicles 16:26.

Faithful preachers will be accused of arrogance because the method and content of their preaching will bear witness to their faith that they are not communicating their own beliefs, but the very words of God.

On the way to church one Sunday morning, I was listening to a local pastor preach on the absolute nature of truth. Yet he kept putting it this way: "I believe truth is absolute."

Listening to him, I kept wincing. Did he know how he sounded? How his very words were at war with each other?

The obvious response to his statement is, "Who cares what you believe? Believe whatever you want—whatever works for you."

Of course I was thankful for his efforts to proclaim the absolute nature of God's truth, but his constant refrain, "I believe," undercut the point he was working so hard to make.

This is our world. We have been inoculated against the very idea of truth and we believe that our individual stories, feelings, and intuitions are truth's highest expression.

Billy Graham was much better at communicating God's authority in his preaching than most pastors today. He'd lift his Bible in his right hand high above his head and say—or rather, declare, "God says," and, "The Bible says." It was never about Billy. It was always about God. It was always about God's Word, His law, and His authority.

### The Apostle Paul's Authority in Athens

Relativism is universal in our world, but it was in the Apostle Paul's world also. Remember the Apostle Paul in Athens? Seeing idols everywhere, Paul told those sophisticated men,

> Men of Athens, I observe that you are very religious in all respects. For while I was passing through and examining the objects of your worship, I also found an altar with this inscription, "TO AN UNKNOWN GOD." Therefore what you worship in ignorance, this I proclaim to you.

I can't help but chuckle at that bit about "ignorance." Can you imagine walking into Harvard Square and using that evangelistic technique?

Paul continued:

> The God who made the world and all things in it, since He is Lord of heaven and earth, does not dwell in temples made with hands; nor is He served by human hands, as though He needed anything, since He Himself gives to all people life and breath and all things; and He made from one man every nation of mankind to live on all the face of the earth, having determined their appointed times and the boundaries of their habitation, that they would seek God, if perhaps they might grope for Him and find Him, though He is not far from each one of us; for in Him we live and move and exist, as even some of your own poets have said, "For we also are His children."

"Grope"? Did the men of Athens think of themselves as "groping"? Would any philosopher use that word today to describe the search for God of the men of the Areopagus in uber-sophisticated Athens?

> Being then the children of God, we ought not to think that the Divine Nature is like gold or silver or stone, an image formed by the art and thought of man.

This was a direct denunciation of the idols that surrounded the Apostle Paul and the men of Athens as he preached to them.

Paul brings his preaching to an end with this terrible insult:

> Therefore having overlooked the times of ignorance, God is now declaring to men that all people everywhere should repent, because He has fixed a day in which He will judge the world in righteousness through a Man whom He has appointed, having furnished proof to all men by raising Him from the dead.[20]

Imagine how dogmatic and arrogant the Apostle Paul's words must have sounded to the Athenians:

20. Acts 17:22–31.

*Yeah, right. Your own god is the only true god. He's the one who made the world and everything in it. He's determined the borders of the Roman Empire. We gave you Aristotle, Socrates, and Plato, but we're groping at truth? We're ignorant?*

*You conceited fool.*

*You tell us unless we repent he'll judge us—and the proof is some guy you claim was raised from the dead?*

*Are you serious?*

People like to point to this passage as the template for modern preaching. But the sad truth is that such preaching is nonexistent inside and outside the church, starting with the fact that the preaching of the Apostle Paul is filled with radical truth statements allowing absolutely no wiggle room.

He didn't preface each sentence with hedge words and weasel expressions like "maybe," "may I suggest to you," "I believe," or "I think." Rather, he declared the truth: the God who made the world and all things in it is Lord of heaven and earth and in Him we live and move and have our being.

Put yourself in the minds of the Athenians listening that day and it's little wonder Scripture tells us "some began to sneer."[21] A man would have to be a fool to say the things Paul said. Then, to top it all off, he began to proclaim the resurrection of the dead.

### Christ's Authority Over the Roman Empire

Moving into the first few centuries following the Apostolic Age, we find Christians were persecuted precisely because of their opposition to the radical relativism in those times.

The Roman Empire encompassed the ancient world. Many countries, races, and ethnic groups were under Rome's rule, so keeping the peace was

---

21. Acts 17:32.

no easy task. One of the greatest challenges the emperors faced was avoiding offending the various gods worshiped by each people group.

Rome solved this problem by being inclusive. The peace of the Roman Empire was built upon a diversity that was embraced religiously and enforced militarily. Instead of demanding her subjects worship Roman gods, Rome endorsed every nation's gods. The pantheon of gods was the law of the Empire and everyone got along with one another just fine as long as no one attacked their neighbor's god. Religious relativism was the fabric of the Roman Empire.

Yet Christians were radically opposed to all idolatry and they bore faithful witness that all the gods of the nations are idols—that their God was the One who alone made the heavens and the earth.[22] The God and Father of the Lord Jesus Christ was the One in whom every man lived and moved and had his being, and one day soon all men would be judged by His Son Jesus.

Can you feel the tension?

You bet you can. Today, it's all around you. Like the Christians of the Roman Empire, we live in a radically inclusive and relativistic world.

Following the ascension of our Lord, the Gospel message grew in its divisiveness. First, believers were persecuted in Jerusalem, then in Judea and Samaria, then to the uttermost parts of the earth. Rome's tolerance did not extend to the rock-hard exclusivity of the preachers of the Christian Gospel—that Jesus is the way, the truth, and the life, and no man comes to the Father except through Him.[23]

When Christians were persecuted, what charges were brought against them?

Two: atheism and anarchy.[24]

Atheism and anarchy? How could that be? The New Testament epistles are filled with commands to love our neighbors, pay our taxes, and respect, submit to, and pray for our rulers.

By the logic of Rome's civil magistrates, though, Christians upset the Empire's delicate balance of gods and their various religions. If believers

---

22. Psalm 96:5.

23. John 14:6.

24. See Herbert Workman, "Caesar or Christ," ch. 2 in *Persecution in the Early Church* (Warhorn Media, 2014).

called all men to faith in Jesus Christ, this was an attack upon Rome's pantheon of gods, and thus an attack upon Rome's peace. Christians were anarchists for attacking the Empire's peace, and they were atheists for rejecting the Empire's gods.

This is the reason Christians were persecuted and martyred. The Gospel was a radically authoritative command given in the glorious name of Almighty God to every man, calling him to turn from his false gods to worship the only true God.

Remember when our Lord said He had come into the world "to testify to the truth"? A cynical ruler in a cosmopolitan, diverse, and inclusive world cynically asked, "What is truth?"[25]

Things have come full circle and Christian preaching is again opposed to the peace of the empire. This time though, the empire isn't Rome. It's the empire of the United States of America. Our *Pax Americana* is built upon the foundation of radical relativism and the state enforces a religious pluralism that is increasingly marginalizing Christians from civilized society.

We don't fit in because we can't fit in if we speak God's words and call men to repent of their rebellion against God's law. Since biblical preaching is the proclamation of the Lordship of Jesus Christ over all His earth, Gospel preachers must be silenced.

Unless, of course, we are able to find a way to split the difference between the authority of the Word of God and our nation's idolatrous relativism.

How and where would we do that?

### The Necessity of Clear Notes

For if the bugle produces an indistinct sound, who will prepare himself for battle?[26]

Find the place where the hatred of our culture for Scripture's doctrine is most intense. Is that the place where the pastor proclaims the teaching of the Word of God with the greatest clarity? Take sex, for instance: Are we most direct and do we preach with the greatest simplicity there? Do we

25. John 18:37–38.
26. 1 Corinthians 14:8.

preach there in clear notes or are we careful to use slightly indistinct sounds?

Today, the clearest test of a church's devotion to the teaching of the apostles is its view on sexuality. You can ask whether the church has women elders and women staffers who attend elders' meetings. You can look at whether women lead mixed-sex home fellowship groups in your church. And yes, by all means notice whether women administer the Lord's Supper to the congregation of your church.

But most of all, we need to listen to our preaching. Do our pastors show zeal to guard the good deposit here at sexuality where Satan has focused his attack on biblical faith? Do we preach that God's Fatherhood is the archetype for man's fatherhood? Do we explain that God's plan for authority in this world is not matriarchy or anarchy, but patriarchy—literally "father-rule"?

Yes, of course we call husbands to love their wives as Christ loved the Church and gave Himself up for her. Men disobey this command and so it should be emphasized.

But no one punishes a pastor for preaching this command and that's why every pastor is zealous to preach this biblical command concerning sexuality.

But honestly, big deal.

The real test of our devotion to the teaching of the apostles is whether we use the pulpit to call the women of the congregation to submit to their husbands. Whether we proclaim the headship of the husband over the wife which flows from Christ's Headship over the Church. Whether, when we mention submission, we soft-sell it by talking about "mutual submission" implying there's an equivalence between husbands submitting to their wives and wives submitting to their husbands.

## Biblical Sexuality Is Not Some "Ideal"

What I've written above is not some "biblical ideal" that's nice to think about and strive for. It is basic Christian faith and practice.

There is a great attack on biblical sexuality today, not simply in connection with father-rule, but in areas such as divorce and remarriage, fruitfulness, age of consent, sodomy, fornication, incest . . . Likely, it won't be long before congregations here in the United States that call sexual sinners to repentance and faith in Jesus Christ will lose their tax-exempt status. Today in many parts of the world, Christians who proclaim biblical sexuality are persecuted and even arrested for hate-speech crimes.

Christian pastors, elders, and writers feel the noose tightening here in North America, and that's why we have stopped proclaiming the teaching of the apostles with authority. Evangelical publishers, colleges, conferences, and churches have become rich by developing perfect pitch when it comes to knowing where the evangelical masses want their ears scratched.

But it was Jesus Himself who said,

Woe to you when all men speak well of you, for their fathers used to treat the false prophets in the same way.[27]

There is no devotion to the teaching of the apostles where preaching lacks authority and clarity at the breach in the wall. Preaching must be authoritative in its content.

Preaching must also be authoritative in its delivery.

### Authority in Delivery

Read our Lord's Sermon on the Mount.[28] Read any of the sermons given in the Book of Acts where the apostles point the finger at their congregations saying, for instance, "You killed Him, but God raised Him from the dead."[29]

A church that is devoted to the apostles' teaching will not tolerate preaching that avoids speaking to the conscience with the same authority that characterized the apostles' preaching. Such preaching is well suited to congregants who expect their pastor to flatter them, but it's not apostolic.

Why?

Because it massages men's egos. It "captivate[s] weak women, burdened with sins and swayed by various impulses."[30]

27. Luke 6:26.
28. Matthew 5–7.
29. See Acts 2:22–24; 4:8–12; 7:51–54.
30. 2 Timothy 3:6.

Like the false prophets of old, it says, "Peace, peace," but there is no peace.[31]

It gives us "yes" and "maybe," but never "no." It tickles the ears of men who will no longer put up with sound doctrine but instead appoint search committees to carefully weed out any man who would be so gauche as to thunder from the pulpit, "Thus says the Lord God Almighty, our worthy Judge eternal!"

By now it should be clear that what passes for preaching in conservative congregations here in North America only rarely bears resemblance to the teaching of the apostles, and for good reason. Men who proclaim God's Word with authority today are scorned, mocked, and hated. It takes faith for a pastor to be devoted to the teaching of the apostles in the pulpit Sunday mornings. It also takes faith for the members of his congregation to be devoted to the teaching of the apostles if he preaches apostolically.

I want to record here something one of my life heroes said once in response to a world-weary and cynical journalist who couldn't understand him and his commitments.

During the years he lived here in these United States, the great prophet against Communism, Aleksandr Solzhenitsyn, knew the sort of man America wanted. Still, he refused to flatter us.

Back in the early nineties during the fall of Communism, Solzhenitsyn decided to return home to his native Russia. During his time in exile here in the United States, he'd not been popular. Starting with his addresses to the AFL–CIO and then Harvard in the late seventies, Solzhenitsyn exposed the moral complacency of his new country, and did so fearlessly.

That was the end of his speaking engagements.

Almost twenty years later as he prepared to return home, the *New Yorker* sent a correspondent up to Solzhenitsyn's farm in Vermont to interview him:

Back in the study, I asked Solzhenitsyn about his relations with the West. He knew that things had gone wrong, but had no intention of making any apologies.

31. Jeremiah 6:14.

"Instead of secluding myself here and writing . . . , I suppose I could have spent time making myself likable to the West," he said. "The only problem is that I would have had to drop my way of life and my work. And, yes, it is true, when I fought the dragon of Communist power I fought it at the highest pitch of expression. The people in the West were not accustomed to this tone of voice. In the West, one must have a balanced, calm, soft voice; one ought to make sure to doubt oneself, to suggest that one may, of course, be completely wrong. But I didn't have the time to busy myself with this. This was not my main goal."[32]

When I first read that, it went off inside me with the power of a nuclear bomb. If a pastor's goal is to be likable, to be given serious consideration by pulpit search committees, to not be taken to task by elders during session meetings, to have peaceful weeks in between Sunday-morning performances of helpful thoughts for the week spiced with biblical erudition, he will work hard to cultivate a certain tone of voice—balanced, calm, and soft. He will be sure to doubt himself, to suggest that he may, of course, be entirely wrong.

But such a man is a false shepherd. He is a betrayer of the sheep Jesus bought with His own blood. Such a man should be brought up on charges for betraying his pastoral calling. He stands condemned and should be fired.

If the Church is to be devoted to the teaching of the apostles, our pastors must turn from fearing man to fearing God. And our churches must love them for it, taking great care to encourage them to keep on in this hard work.

---

32. David Remnick, "The Exile Returns," *New Yorker*, February 14, 1994, 74.

*For out of much affliction and anguish of heart I wrote to you with many tears; not so that you would be made sorrowful, but that you might know the love which I have especially for you.*

—2 Corinthians 2:4

# CHAPTER 4

# *Fellowship*

**T**HE CHURCH'S SECOND CORPORATE DEVO-
tion is fellowship. The church in Jerusalem was devoted to their
common life together. The Greek word *koinōnia* is translated "fellowship" in the New Testament, and like the English word "church" the word
"fellowship" has taken on a certain spiritual flavor. What do you think of
when you hear the word "fellowship"?

The range of meanings *koinōnia* had in Greek when it was used by the
apostles (nineteen times in the New Testament) extended from contribu-
tion to association, community, and intimacy. In other words, there is a lot
more to fellowship than church potlucks.

### Intimacy Is Hard Work

We will find in our examination of the four devotions that each is difficult
and their difficulty requires us to be devoted to them. We think of fellowship as warm and fuzzy, but actually it's hard. Outside the grace of the Holy
Spirit, intimacy can be intolerable.

Married couples divorce because intimacy is difficult. It's hard to remain intimate with a slob. It's hard to remain intimate with a shrew. It's hard to remain intimate with a drunk or a narcissist or a sixty-year-old man still complaining that his mother didn't love him.

People leave small groups and churches because of intimacy. It's hard to listen to someone confess for the seventy-seventh time that he's looked at strange flesh on his computer. It's hard to sit through the seventy-seventh iteration of a man in your small group whining about how much he doesn't like his job and how unfair his boss is and how smart he is and how depressing it is for his smartness not to be appreciated by his boss and how next month things will be different because he has a line on a new job and does anyone have an extra car they can loan his wife because hers is in the shop and . . .

Fellowship requires patience, humility, and honesty. Fellowship also requires money, homes, and food. Fellowship is costly, yet without fellowship a church denies the Gospel and has no love for God. We prove our love for God by loving our brothers and sisters in the church. In the gospel of John we are told, "By this all men will know that you are my disciples, if you have love for one another."[1]

Just as God the Father, God the Son, and God the Holy Spirit have fellowship with One Another, so God has placed man, His image bearer, in relationships for fellowship with one another.

## What True Fellowship Looks Like

It was never God's intent for us to live in loneliness and alienation. Our separation from Him and one another is the result of sin—both Adam's and our own—but God who is rich in mercy has made a way for us to have our fellowship with Him and one another restored. The path of restoration is through His Son, Jesus Christ. God made us for fellowship, and when God gives us faith and calls us out to be His Church, He restores the intimacy of fellowship to us—fellowship with God and fellowship with one another through Him:

1. John 13:35.

... what we have seen and heard we proclaim to you also, so that you too may have fellowship with us; and indeed our fellowship is with the Father, and with His Son Jesus Christ ...

... if we walk in the Light as He Himself is in the Light, we have fellowship with one another, and the blood of Jesus His Son cleanses us from all sin.[2]

We see a beautiful portrayal of that restoration in Acts where we read of the devotion to fellowship that characterized the first church in Jerusalem:

And all those who had believed were together, and had all things in common; and they began selling their property and possessions, and were sharing them with all, as anyone might have need. Day by day continuing with one mind in the temple, and breaking bread from house to house, they were taking their meals together with gladness and sincerity of heart, praising God, and having favor with all the people. And the Lord was adding to their number day by day those who were being saved.[3]

All through this account of the first days of the first Christian church, we see evidence that their fellowship was deep. As soon as they were baptized, each of the souls was "added" to the church of Jerusalem and they were continually devoting themselves to "fellowship."

What was this "fellowship" like? How did it look to the watching world?

The believers were "together," they "had all things in common," they shared their property, possessions, and money; they were of "one mind" and "together" in the temple, they went "from house to house" taking their meals "together."

With this quality of intimacy and love, it is no surprise that "the Lord was adding to their number day by day those who were being saved." Would it be possible to have the same quality of fellowship in our churches today? Should we even hope for it?

2. 1 John 1:3, 7.
3. Acts 2:44–47.

God made us to love Him and to love one another—these are the two greatest commandments.

Note how John, the apostle of love, links fellowship with God and fellowship with one another:

> What we have seen and heard we proclaim to you also, so that you too may have fellowship with us; and indeed our fellowship is with the Father, and with His Son Jesus Christ. These things we write, so that our joy may be made complete.[4]

What joy there is in the life of the Christian who has fellowship with God and his brothers and sisters in Christ. If you've ever been a part of a church that, united in the true doctrine of the apostles, lives in harmony and tenderness, you find your heart burning within you when you read portions of Scripture such as Psalm 133:

> Behold, how good and how pleasant it is
> For brothers to dwell together in unity!
> It is like the precious oil upon the head,
> Coming down upon the beard,
> Even Aaron's beard,
> Coming down upon the edge of his robes.
> It is like the dew of Hermon
> Coming down upon the mountains of Zion;
> For there the LORD commanded the blessing—life forever.

We were made for fellowship, and being united with Christ calls us into the church where, by God's grace, "brothers dwell together in unity."

But then we run into a snag. "Fellowship" is a word used quite a bit in churches today, but the sort of occasions and relationships it's used to refer to seem lukewarm compared to what we see in the church in Jerusalem:

> "Fellowship" is an overworked word in the contemporary church, and the image conveyed by it is often a false image. Indeed, the vocabulary

4. 1 John 1:3–4.

of fellowship has become such devalued currency that it seldom means
more than a genial mateyness, . . . or a good gossipy get-together over
a nice cup of tea [or coffee].[5]

Even our reference works have a cheapened view of fellowship. For
instance, a thesaurus will suggest "affability," "camaraderie," and "friendly intercourse" as synonyms. But the fellowship of the first church called
*koinōnia* by Luke is meant to communicate the "joining of themselves
together" or the "holding of things in common." That raises the ante,
doesn't it?

In other words, believers in the first church applied themselves to being
connected and committed to each other. Sharing their money and possessions wasn't early socialism or communism. It was merely the fruit of
mutual love.

Here I should insert a cautionary note: fellowship is not a natural human skill that can be pursued in the flesh. Fellowship never comes about
simply through the well-intentioned efforts of good people. It is a gift of
God accomplished only through the power of His perfect love being "shed
abroad" among us.[6]

The fellowship we share as Christians doesn't come from some great
ability to "imagine" a "new age" in which "all men are brothers." It isn't
random acts of kindness breaking out from sentimental goodwill among
people who have listened to John Lennon and caught the dream of the
world living "as one."

Christian fellowship and brotherly love only come out of the total trans-
formation of our spirits of flesh by God's Holy Spirit. Adopted by our heavenly Father, we are taught by Him to love one another as He first loved us.

Through the Holy Spirit's call and gifts, followers of Jesus Christ are
built into a new family, the family of God, which has as its very center the
Lamb of God pouring out His life for us on the cross. To talk of Christian
fellowship as a thing that can happen among men and women who hav-
en't publicly confessed their faith and been baptized into the Church is a
perversion of the word. Any communion that occurs between those who,

5. John Stott, *One People* (InterVarsity Press, 1968), 69.
6. Romans 5:5 (KJV).

living in rebellion against God, reject incorporation into His family is a sickly copy of the harmony and intimacy God gives His children within His Church.

This means our conversations at church potlucks or home fellowship groups should be deeper than conversations in the break room at work, the gym, on the subway, or at the coffee shop. The racial and socioeconomic inclusivity of the Church puts to shame the counterfeits of the "inclusivity" the progressive world boasts of and passes laws to enforce. Our acceptance of people from other races, with other physical conditions, with higher or lower levels of educational or financial accomplishment, is spontaneous and carefree—not forced by social pressure or administrative and legal threats.

It is said that the true test of a nation's government is how it protects its poor and weak—illegal aliens and the unborn, for instance—those at the margins of life who can't protect themselves. In a similar way, the true test of the Church's fellowship and love is at the margins of her life among those who don't fit in any way other than that they also are our heavenly Father's sons and daughters. This is what the Apostle Paul is referring to when he writes,

> There is neither Jew nor Greek, there is neither slave nor free man, there is neither male nor female; for you are all one in Christ Jesus.[7]

We are all one in Christ Jesus.

Today, one of the best tests of the quality of a particular church's fellowship is to look at whether there are people there who don't look like they belong. Are there men and women outside of the demographic composition of the church's dominant group? Are there men and women who don't "fit," and are they the ones who receive our most tender care and love?

If you're a part of a white southern church with "First" in its name—First Presbyterian or First Baptist for instance—are there any African Americans in your congregation?

---

7. Galatians 3:28.

## Good Church, Bad Church

One of the churches where I have worshiped with my family and been encouraged is London's Metropolitan Tabernacle (the "Tab") where Charles Spurgeon served many years ago. The order of worship and songs seemed to come straight from Spurgeon's time, and, though the preacher wasn't Spurgeon, his sermon was still solid meat for the mature. Prior to the call to worship, the congregation was cheerful without being profane. People greeted and obviously liked one another, but they were there to worship Almighty God, and there was an obvious reverence as they filled in the pews.

The sanctuary was simplicity itself: no decorative items, no banners, no plants on the platform, no stained-glass windows, no pompous bulletin, no plexiglass pulpit—and certainly no Starbucks counter.

The moment we had exited the Tube at Elephant Castle and started walking to the Tab in the rain, it was clear the whole enterprise would be humble. The Elephant Castle station is drab, the neighborhood is drab, and, when you get there, the Tab is drab too—visually, that is.

But during the service, the participation of the congregation in the singing and prayer was heartfelt. Clearly each soul present expected to meet God in His Word as the sermon was preached. (Pastors sense these things.)

Now at this point you may be wondering why I found it especially encouraging. Surely I've been in other churches where the worship was reverent, the congregation participated with their hearts, and the Word of God was honored?

What I haven't told you is that the white people in the congregation were a distinct minority. There were many, many Asians, many Pakistanis and Indians, and quite a few blacks. It was a congregation of color.

Why did this make me joyful?

Because there was neither Jew nor Greek, slave nor free, male nor female, but we were all one in Christ.

After the service, our family shared in table fellowship with an Indian man and his family who invited us home for dinner. He was an elder and he lowered himself to serve a Yankee family.

Contrast that with our attendance at Evensong that night in St. Paul's Cathedral—the highest expression of Anglicanism London has to offer. If the Tab was a rainbow of color, St. Paul's was white, white, white.

A magnificent structure on the outside, it was even more so on the inside. Walking through the doors one felt a sense of having arrived: here was profundity, order, art, and a sense of historic moment greater than anything so petty and small as a fisherman preaching the Gospel. This was nothing less than the British Empire in microcosm.

But the congregation and worship? Drab, actually. Few actually sang the hymns, and if anyone tried (as our family did), the magnificent pipe organ drowned them out. But it was a show P. T. Barnum would have envied.

The man who officiated presented to the congregation the most ostentatious rendition of the word "God" I'd ever heard. He transmogrified it into seven syllables.

Afterwards, our youngest son Taylor tried to find a bathroom. Very politely, Taylor asked one of the functionaries if there was a bathroom he could please use.

Showing Taylor to the street, the man told him there was a public bathroom down the road that might be open. But it was late enough Sunday evening that this city facility was closed.

"Too bad," he said to Taylor when he returned, "but there's no helping it."

We had worshiped with them, been a part of some sort of ritual of passing the peace using water, sung to the glory of the Lord Jesus Christ, heard the Word read, listened to the homily, yet when a visiting boy needed to use the bathroom they would not permit it.

Now you may think I'm making too big a deal about this, but contrast the reception we had at St. Paul's with the reception we had that morning at Spurgeon's Metropolitan Tabernacle.

The Tab was a true house of God. Though possessed of a greater spiritual heritage than St. Paul's, the Tab was no museum, but a house of God where true love, true fellowship, true sharing among God's people took place. Fellowship was as central to the worship of that glorious church as the authority of God's Word. When true Christian fellowship is present in a church, it's obvious. And when it's absent, it's equally obvious.

## Sharing Our Lives

Some people want a church without fellowship. They want to get in and out, doing church as efficiently as possible. Churches large and small cater to them. (Yes, many small churches are as careful to avoid knowing their sheep as large churches.) But those who know Jesus Christ and love Him can't help but love His people. Our love for one another is irrepressible.

To say it most clearly, the love and sharing relationships of brothers and sisters and mothers and fathers in Christ should make all other human relationships pale by comparison.

I think, though, that if we look honestly at our lives and relationships, most of us see that this is not true. We would admit, for instance, that we will be loyal to our human bloodlines long after our loyalty to our spiritual bloodlines has been broken. We would acknowledge that we feel a greater sense of communion or fellowship with the guys we play basketball or softball with, or the women in our book club, than the people we sit next to in worship.

True Christian fellowship is present when we are more inclined to go to our elders or their wives and ask for help in handling a family crisis, than to a friend who is an unbeliever. Devotion to fellowship is real when the bonds of loyalty bind most tightly within the family of God.

Francis Schaeffer put it this way:

[We are called by God] to practice simultaneously the orthodoxy of doctrine and the orthodoxy of community in the visible church. The latter of these we have too often all but forgotten. But one cannot explain the explosive dynamite . . . of the early church apart from the fact that they practiced two things simultaneously: orthodoxy of doctrine and orthodoxy of community in the midst of the visible church, a community which the world could see. By the grace of God, therefore, the church must be known simultaneously for its purity of doctrine and the reality of its community. Our churches have so often been only preaching points with very little emphasis on community. But exhibition of the love of God in practice is beautiful and must be there.[8]

8. Francis Schaeffer, *The Church Before the Watching World*, reprinted in *A Christian View of the Church*, 2nd ed. (Crossway, 1985), 152.

As I said, intimacy is hard work. Note that Jesus gives the world, the unbelievers, permission to judge whether or not we are truly His disciples on the basis of our love for one another:

> A new commandment I give to you, that you love one another, even as I have loved you, that you also love one another. By this all men will know that you are My disciples, if you have love for one another.[9]

Note Jesus also says the world will judge whether or not He has been sent by God on the basis of the unity of the Body of Christ:

> I do not ask on behalf of these alone, but for those also who believe in Me through their word; that they may all be one; even as You, Father, are in Me and I in You, that they also may be in Us, so that the world may believe that You sent Me.[10]

Christian fellowship is taking a personal interest in one another; sharing heart-to-heart one another's joys and sorrows,

> so that there may be no division in the body, but that the members may have the same care for one another. And if one member suffers, all the members suffer with it; if one member is honored, all the members rejoice with it.[11]

Christian fellowship is also knowing about and helping one another in our physical needs. The New Testament records that collections for the poor were at the heart of the Early Church's fellowship, and this inspires us to do the same today, sharing our food, clothing, and money.

After the breaking of bread in our congregation's Sunday-morning worship, we take a second offering "for the needs of the poor among us." Every Christian should take joy in giving money to help his brothers and sisters in Christ with financial needs. In the Jerusalem church, there was so

9. John 13:34–35.
10. John 17:20–21.
11. 1 Corinthians 12:25–26.

much fellowship of this concrete and practical nature that Acts 6 records seven church officers called "deacons" being called and ordained entirely for this purpose.

Another part of the Church's devotion to fellowship is carried out in what today we often call small groups or home fellowship groups. Such home groups are nothing new. Back at the time of the Reformation, Calvin's associate in Strasbourg despaired of getting the support of the city magistrates to establish real pastoral care and discipline for the entire church, so he put together voluntary groups within the church for those desiring this true fellowship:

> These "Christian fellowships" (*Christliche Gemeinschaften*) were essentially rolls of freely enlisted parishioners who submitted themselves to precisely the kind of disciplinary scrutiny that in *True Pastoral Care* Bucer still aspired to have applied to the whole baptized population.[12]

Centuries later, George Whitefield, called God's people to devote themselves to this same form of fellowship:

> Brothers and sisters, let us plainly and freely tell each other what God has done for our souls. To accomplish this you would do well to follow what others have done and to form yourselves into little companies of four or five and meet once a week to tell each other what is in your hearts, so that you can pray for and comfort each other as (each of you has a need). No one except one who has experienced this can tell the unspeakable advantages of such a union and communion of souls.

Then he adds this exhortation concerning the importance of such fellowship to the well-being of the Church:

> I don't think that anyone who really loves his own soul and his brothers as himself will be shy of opening his heart so that he may have their

---

12. David F. Wright, "Historical Introduction" in Martin Bucer, *Concerning the True Care of Souls* (1538), trans. Peter Beale (Banner of Truth, 2009), xxi.

advice, reproof, admonition, and prayers as occasions require. A sincere person will count this time as one of the greatest blessings.[13]

A decade ago, Pastor Max Curell came to the conviction that our congregation wasn't devoting ourselves to fellowship as we ought. There weren't occasions each week for us to confess our sins, pray, and bear one another's burdens, so he brought a proposal to the elders. There are only so many days in a week and we already had a Wednesday-night education program for the family, so Pastor Max suggested the elders cancel one of our two Sunday worship services and use the time for home fellowship groups.

It was a radical proposal for a number of reasons, including the simple fact that Sunday-evening worship had always been the happiest time of our congregational life. I liked Sunday evenings best of our services, partly because on Sunday evenings we allowed for questions and discussion during the sermon, something we did not have time for on Sunday mornings. We also took prayer requests and members of the congregation prayed for one another during Sunday-evening worship which, again, we didn't do on Sunday morning. It was normal for college and grad students and families to come early and stay late after Sunday-evening worship, often closing down the building almost two hours after the service was over. So why did we stop?

Maybe you've heard the expression that the good is the enemy of the best?

Pastor Curell explained to us that 200–250 was too big for the sort of intimate fellowship our church now needed. We had a bunch of young Christians who had grown up in broken homes with dads and moms who had divorced and they needed a level of personal care we couldn't provide Sunday evenings in a large group. Smaller groups in the intimacy of a family home would permit care and training within an atmosphere of love which was impossible to create in the larger group setting. Small groups would also serve better as a venue for leadership training and provide a consistent first line of care for many of the congregation's needs.

The elders saw the wisdom of this proposal and announced the change

13. Paraphrase of Whitefield's words in his *Letter to the Religious Societies* as quoted in John Stott, *One People*, 88.

to the church. Some were indignant and left. My pastoral judgment was that a number of those we lost were averse to true fellowship—any connection to their brothers and sisters in Christ which went deeper than superficiality.

The first week of home fellowship groups we had ninety-five to a hundred percent participation, and over the years participation has stayed that high. It's true, some groups are better than others, and, despite the decentralization of pastoral care, there are problems that slip through the cracks. But what a tremendous thing to have a church devoted to the fellowship of the saints where we share the joy of those in the first church in Jerusalem who "from house to house . . . were taking their meals together with gladness and sincerity of heart, praising God, and having favor with all the people."[14]

At this point, I can almost hear objections of those cold-fish sort of people—including many pastors and elders—who have little love for the flock and would prefer others not know them. *But how can you control the doctrine of what's being taught if the pastor isn't there to make sure it's safe? If elders aren't leading the discussion, what sort of training do you give the men who are? Are they at least deacons? Is there any authority in these groups, or are they just a bunch of people saying how they feel about what the Bible says or what the preacher said in his sermon?*

And if people knew our church constantly has about one hundred children five years old and under, they would further ask, *What on earth do you do with the children while the adults are sharing and praying?* These are all good questions that I'll answer with the simple maxim, "Where there's a will, there's a way."

Why do we have the will?

Because we see that the church of Jerusalem was devoted to fellowship, a fellowship about as intimate as it could be, and all under the authority of the pastors and elders, because, among other things, in Acts 20 we read that even the Apostle Paul was "night and day" going "from house to house" teaching and admonishing and warning "with tears."[15]

We felt we would not be faithful pastors and elders if we didn't copy this pattern, so we did and we still do today.

14. Acts 2:46–47.
15. Acts 20:20, 31.

Let's bring this chapter on fellowship to a close with an excerpt from Dietrich Bonhoeffer's masterpiece on church life, *Life Together*:

Because God has already laid the only foundation of our fellowship, because God has bound us together in one body with other Christians in Jesus Christ, long before we entered into common life with them, we enter into that common life not as demanders but as thankful recipients. We thank God for what He has done for us. We thank God for giving us brethren who live by His call, by His forgiveness, and His promise. We do not complain of what God does not give us; we rather thank God for what He does give us daily. . . .

. . . If we do not give thanks daily for the Christian fellowship in which we have been placed, even where there is no great experience, no discoverable riches, but much weakness, small faith, and difficulty; if on the contrary, we only keep complaining to God that everything is so paltry and petty, so far from what we expected, then we hinder God from letting our fellowship grow according to the measure and riches which are there for us all in Jesus Christ.[16]

16. Dietrich Bonhoeffer, *Life Together*, trans. John W. Doberstein (HarperCollins, 1954), 28, 29.

*Day by day continuing with one mind in the temple, and breaking bread from house to house, they were taking their meals together with gladness and sincerity of heart.*

*—Acts 2:46*

# CHAPTER 5

# The Breaking
of Bread

**W**E HAVE EXAMINED THE FIRST TWO DEVO-
tions of the Church, the teaching of the apostles and fellowship.
Now let's turn to the third, the "breaking of bread."

What is meant by this phrase?

Breaking of bread is the meal the Church eats together in obedience to
Jesus' command, "Do this in remembrance of me," spoken when He was
with his disciples in the upper room for the Passover meal the night before
He was crucified. Luke describes what happened:

And when He had taken some bread and given thanks, He broke it
and gave it to them, saying, "This is My body which is given for you;
do this in remembrance of Me." And in the same way He took the cup
after they had eaten, saying, "This cup which is poured out for you is
the new covenant in My blood.[1]

1. Luke 22:19–20.

Many congregations have the words, "Do This in Remembrance of Me," inscribed on a table at the front of the sanctuary and serve this meal from that table. Usually the table is front and center, directly under the pulpit devoted to the teaching of the apostles.

What is the meaning of this holy meal?

The Apostle Paul explains, "For as often as you eat this bread and drink the cup, you proclaim the Lord's death until He comes."[2]

Today, God's called-out ones continue to gather for the "teaching of the apostles" and the "breaking of bread." Through these two devotions our worship announces God's good news in Word (preaching) and sacrament (breaking of bread).

Why call the breaking of bread a "sacrament"?

"Sacrament" comes to us from the Latin word *sacramentum* meaning "mystery." The Westminster Shorter Catechism explains,

> A sacrament is a holy ordinance instituted by Christ; wherein, by sensible signs, Christ, and the benefits of the new covenant, are represented, sealed, and applied to believers.[3]

Sacraments are the Gospel in "sensible signs." They are God's good news communicated and applied through things we can see and touch. In the sacraments God lowers Himself to our weakness by dealing with us through physical signs.

Jesus commanded His called-out ones to observe two physical signs. The first is baptism, the Church's initiation rite. The second is the Lord's Supper, the Church's family meal.

Before approaching the specific meaning of the sacrament of the Lord's Supper, we need to understand something about sacraments in general. Sacraments gain meaning only by defining a division. They are meaningless when universally applied. In other words, sacraments only do the work God ordained them for when some may participate and some may not.

The sacraments are precious to us precisely because they physically

2. 1 Corinthians 11:26.

3. Westminster Shorter Catechism, Answer 92, accessed March 11, 2019, https://reformed.org /documents/wsc/index.html.

mark us as God's called-out ones. But if all men and women are baptized and everyone who wants is allowed to eat at the Lord's Table, no one is called out and the sacrament loses its meaning as a positive statement about Christ's elect.

The sacraments are designed to physically clarify the lines between those inside and those outside Christ's Church. Sadly, many pastors and elders today are disobedient and refuse to submit to that design. Thus the sacraments have become one of the most frequent tools of deception in the life of Christ's Church today.

You want to be baptized? Sure, right this way. Happy to oblige!

You want to take the Lord's Supper? Sure, saunter up to the table, and happy to oblige!

Faithful shepherds understand the temptation to use baptism and communion to make a show of religion or spirituality, and they forbid it. The holy things of God should never be abused for man's sinful purposes.

The sacraments are only a precious comfort to us when they mark our bodies in such a way as to be a sign and seal that God has called us out from the world to be His own.

Now then, five things we need to be clear on in connection with the sacrament of the Lord's Supper:

1. The Lord's Supper is for God's called-out ones whose faith is in Jesus Christ.
2. The Lord's Supper does not belong to individuals or families, but to the Church.
3. The Lord's Supper is a meal of Christian unity.
4. The Lord's Supper must not be approached superstitiously.
5. The Lord's Supper is for sinners.

### The Lord's Supper is for God's called-out ones whose faith is in Jesus Christ.

When we warn unbelievers against participating in the Lord's Supper, it is called "fencing the table." Many churches today state no such warnings.

Pastors neither warn nor bar anyone from the Lord's Table, but instead the souls present are invited and even pressured to participate.

Thus unbelievers and the unrepentant eat this holy meal without examining themselves, turning it into a sham and endangering themselves both spiritually and physically.

Why do I say "examining themselves"? Because in 1 Corinthians, Paul gives this command:

> Whoever eats the bread or drinks the cup of the Lord in an unworthy manner, shall be guilty of the body and the blood of the Lord. But a man must examine himself, and in so doing he is to eat of the bread and drink of the cup. For he who eats and drinks, eats and drinks judgment to himself if he does not judge the body rightly. For this reason many among you are weak and sick, and a number sleep [have died].[4]

Listen to the Apostle Paul's rebuke of this same Corinthian congregation for allowing an unrepentant man to be in their church and communing with them:

> It is actually reported that there is immorality among you, and immorality of such a kind as does not exist even among the Gentiles, that someone has his father's wife. You have become arrogant, and have not mourned instead, in order that the one who had done this deed might be removed from your midst.[5]

The Apostle Paul rebukes the Corinthians for allowing this man to remain a part of their communion, and what does he tell them to do? He commands them to remove the man:

> Do you not judge those who are within the church? But those who are outside, God judges. Remove the wicked man from among yourselves.[6]

---

4. 1 Corinthians 11:27–30.
5. 1 Corinthians 5:1–2.
6. 1 Corinthians 5:12–13.

"Remove the wicked man." At the heart of a congregation's biblical duties is their responsibility to judge those within the church. They are to expel any man who calls himself a brother and is found to be immoral or covetous; a swindler, idolater, reviler, or drunkard.[7] It was a terrible failure of the church in Corinth that they had not removed this man committing incest from their worship and communion.

Now let me ask a question so obvious we could miss it.

How can the elders of the Corinthian church expel a man they have no authority over? What does it mean to expel him if he can continue to eat the Lord's Supper with them and there's nothing they can do about it?

Think about it: the Lord's Supper is the family meal of the household of faith, and a man living in unrepentant sin has no place at that table. Such a man must be barred from profaning the body and blood of our Lord, and this is the duty of a church's officers—her pastor and elders.

Barring and removing unbelievers and unrepentant sinners from sharing in the Lord's Supper is the most basic exercise of the authority God has given the fathers of His household for the protection of God's holy name and the souls for whom Jesus died. Allowing notorious sinners to eat and drink of these holy things tramples on the body and blood of our Lord. It also causes a scandal that leads the sheep astray and causes shipwreck to their souls.

But the pastor and elders have been delegated authority for the protection of this sinner, also. The words of the Apostle Paul make it clear that a goal of discipline is to lead the sinner to repentance so that, in time, he may be restored to table fellowship.[8] It's simple, isn't it?

Those called by God to exercise authority within the Church must not abdicate that authority. Failing to call sinners to repentance leads not only to the destruction of sinners, but causes the spreading of leaven throughout the family of God and leads unbelievers to blaspheme the name of our Lord Jesus Christ.

7. 1 Corinthians 5:11.
8. If the historic understanding of 2 Corinthians 2:5–8 is correct, the man living in incest was granted repentance and the Corinthians had the joy of restoring him to the Church's fellowship and communion.

## The Lord's Supper does not belong to individuals or families, but to the Church.

One of the most frequent causes of visitors not returning to our church is the simple statement we make every time we fence the Lord's Table.[9]

Although our congregation practices "open communion,"[10] those who approach the table to eat and drink must "be members of an evangelical or Bible-believing church." Which is to say, those who refuse to submit to the instruction and discipline of the officers of Christ's Church are barred from our table fellowship.

If men and women refuse to place themselves under the authority and discipline of a particular church's shepherds, they are out in the wilderness wandering in terrible danger with absolutely no protection from the undershepherds God has called to guide and guard them. Were the elders of our congregation to allow them to come and eat the Lord's Supper while they remained in this condition, they would be conniving at their sin and would be responsible for their blood.

So why are people offended by this? Because in our individualistic American culture there is a common belief that the Table of our Lord is Jesus' gift to the individual believer directly, and no man has the right to bar anyone from communing with Jesus there.

Is this true? Has our Lord given this sacrament directly to individuals?

No. This meal is not an individual religious exercise. It is the family meal for God's adopted sons and daughters. This meal has nothing to do with me-and-Jesus individualism. The Lord's Supper is given to the Church as a sign and seal of membership in His covenant community.

---

9. To "fence the table" is the duty of the church officer administering the sacrament to declare who is and who is not allowed to come to the table, and why. Scripture makes this duty clear in 1 Corinthians 11:17–34.

10. "Open communion" is the practice followed by most churches and denominations today of welcoming other believers to join with them in the celebration of the Lord's Supper, despite not holding membership in their own church or denomination. "Closed communion" is the practice of the Roman Catholic Church and denominations such as the Lutheran Church–Missouri Synod. These churches welcome only those who hold membership in their own fellowship.

Every church should fence the Lord's Table, welcoming only those who are members of a particular evangelical or Bible-believing church.

We must never cede the household meal to ignorant or rebellious individuals who reject the Bride Christ loves, living as prodigals exposed to every danger sent them by the Devil.

### The Lord's Supper is a meal of Christian unity.

Scripture condemns the celebration of this meal when it is served in such a way as to deny or destroy the unity of the Church. God cares very much about the unity of His household, and it is the duty of the officers He has placed over His household to govern it in such a way as to protect that unity.[11]

In Corinth, church members were sinning against this unity. The believers in Corinth were divided as a congregation and this division was evident in a host of ways. They were proud of their superiority to each other intellectually. They were proud while a man in their midst was committing incest with his father's wife. They were peacocks parading their spiritual gift of tongues before others. They were taking each other to court, asking pagan judges to settle their disputes.

Their congregation was filled with division, yet they came to break bread together, acting as if they were at peace with one another as the Body of Christ. Division among them was so bad that some of them made a conspicuous display of their wealth by pigging out and getting drunk on their own abundance, while others breaking bread with them had nothing to eat or drink.

Can you imagine?

As an officer of God's household,[12] the Apostle Paul rebuked them for this disunity. He wrote the Corinthians,

11. 1 Timothy 3:2, 4–5: "He [an elder] must be one who manages his own household well, keeping his children under control with all dignity (but if a man does not know how to manage his own household, how will he take care of the church of God?)."

12. 1 Timothy 3:15: "I write so that you may know how one ought to conduct himself in the household of God, which is the church of the living God, the pillar and support of the truth."

But in giving this instruction, I do not praise you, because you come
together not for the better but for the worse. For, in the first place, when
you come together as a church, I hear that divisions exist among you.
... Therefore when you meet together, it is not to eat the Lord's Supper,
for in your eating each one takes his own supper first; and one is hungry
and another is drunk. What! Do you not have houses in which to eat
and drink? Or do you despise the church of God, and shame those who
have nothing? What shall I say to you? Shall I praise you? In this I will
not praise you. . . . So then, my brethren, when you come together to
eat, wait for one another.[13]

Their division was so awful that the Apostle Paul's rebuke declared their
celebration of the Lord's Supper to be "for the worse." In other words, it
would have been better if they had not celebrated the Lord's Supper at all!

Why?

Because, the Apostle Paul said, their pride and division showed they
"despise the church of God."

Paul's statement makes clear that God has given the Lord's Supper to the
Church as a corporate sacrament. He did not give it to individual Christians
or their families. The church around the table is to be one body, and the
Apostle Paul dealt with the division in the Corinthian church with stark
and rigid language.

First, in verse 22 he condemns their sin:

What! Do you not have houses in which to eat and drink? Or do you
despise the church of God, and shame those who have nothing? What
shall I say to you? Shall I praise you? In this I will not praise you.

Then come the words of institution read each time we observe this
sacrament, which begin, "For I received from the Lord that which I also
delivered unto you, that the Lord Jesus in the night in which he was be-
trayed took bread . . ."[14]

13. 1 Corinthians 11:17–18, 20–22, 33.
14. See 1 Corinthians 11:23–26.

But immediately following the words of institution, he returns to his warning and rebuke:

> Therefore whoever eats the bread or drinks the cup of the Lord in an unworthy manner, shall be guilty of the body and the blood of the Lord. But let a man examine himself, and so let him eat of the bread and drink of the cup. For he who eats and drinks, eats and drinks judgment to himself, if he does not judge the body rightly. For this reason many among you are weak and sick, and a number sleep. But if we judged ourselves rightly, we should not be judged. But when we are judged, we are disciplined by the Lord in order that we may not be condemned along with the world.
>
> So then, my brethren, when you come together to eat, wait for one another. If anyone is hungry, let him eat at home, so that you may not come together for judgment. And the remaining matters I shall arrange when I come.[15]

The Apostle Paul says the result of God's fatherly discipline in the Corinthian church has been that many among them were "weak and sick, and a number sleep [have died]."

Paul goes on to explain how to avoid such discipline. The church in Corinth must examine and judge themselves so they will not be "guilty of the body and blood of the Lord."

What sin are they to look for?

They are to look for division and take steps against it. Specifically, concerning the parading of their wealth by some, they are to "wait for one another"—the same theme struck earlier in the chapter—and if they are hungry, they are to "eat at home."

Taking the Apostle Paul's warning to heart, what would we look for in a particular congregation which would indicate sensitivity to the importance of unity around the table?

Look for exhortations related to unity and division during the words

15. 1 Corinthians 11:27–34.

of preparation. Does the pastor allow time for souls to go and make things right with others? Remember our Lord's warning about this matter?

> You have heard that the ancients were told, "You shall not commit murder" and "Whoever commits murder shall be liable to the court." But I say to you that everyone who is angry with his brother shall be guilty before the court; and whoever shall say to his brother, "You good-for-nothing," shall be guilty before the supreme court; and whoever says, "You fool," shall be guilty enough to go into the fiery hell. Therefore if you are presenting your offering at the altar, and there remember that your brother has something against you, leave your offering there before the altar and go; first be reconciled to your brother, and then come and present your offering.[16]

Where might we see signs of unity or disunity in the Church today?

Go to a congregational meeting and take the temperature of the congregation in that place and time where congregational divisions are most likely to surface. What is the spirit of the meeting? Is it sweet, or rather angry and bitter? Is love evident? Do members speak with gentleness and affection for one another? When they disagree, is it obvious they trust one another?

Go into the kitchen and see if there's dust on the plates. A peaceful and loving congregation eats together.

Time how long it takes for the parking lot to empty after Sunday-morning worship. If people hang out a long while talking after the service, it's likely they love one another.

These are just hints in the direction of checking for unity or division in a congregation. You will no doubt come up with your own methods of discerning this vital aspect of church life.

One final caution: both sacraments God has given us—baptism and the Lord's Supper—are corporate. As I said in the chapter on baptism, they are not personal and they ought not to be administered privately.[17] One of the

---

16. Matthew 5:21–24.
17. The Westminster Confession of Faith, 29.3–4, condemns private administrations of the Lord's Supper: it is to be administered "to none who are not then present in the congregation. Private masses, or receiving this sacrament by a priest, or any other alone, . . . are all contrary to the nature of this sac-

more frequent violations of this biblical principle in the administration of the Lord's Supper is its celebration during wedding ceremonies where the bride and groom are served, but no one else.

This should not be. The Lord's Supper is a visible demonstration of the unity of the Body of Christ under the cross of Christ. It is not given to us to provide weddings a special spiritual ethos that the congregation merely observes.

## The Lord's Supper must not be approached superstitiously.

Throughout church history and across the world today, two errors have been common among those receiving the Lord's Supper: first, the error of considering it "only a memorial meal" for the purpose of being reminded of our Lord's death; and second, the error of considering it a means of grace without regard to the faith of the one communing.

First, let's look at the error of the "memorial only" view. A couple of times I've found myself in the awkward position of being present when the Lord's Supper was served outside the corporate worship of a church by well-meaning souls who thought it would lend a certain spiritual gravity to what was going on at the time. Both occasions caught me by surprise and I fought a great internal conflict over whether or not to participate.

The first occasion was back thirty years ago when I was asked to preside at a wedding ceremony by a young woman who was a friend of our family. She was marrying a young man in training for pastoral ministry. At the conclusion of the wedding rehearsal held in another church in a nearby community (not the church I served), this man announced to those of us assembled at the front of the church that we would conclude the rehearsal with "communion."

The second time, my wife and I were attending a meeting of a para-

---

rament, and to the institution of Christ." Nevertheless, an exception can be made in the case of a sick person unable to come to church for an extended period of time. In such a case, I recommend taking a few people representing the fellowship of the congregation along to the sick person's home, so that the administration of the Lord's Supper to him is not a private affair.

church campus ministry where there was preaching, prayer, songs—much of what is normally included in a corporate worship service—but tacked on to the end of the service was what they called "communion." Again, I faced the decision whether or not to participate.

Maybe you've had a similar experience at a summer camp or youth retreat following a campfire talk by one of your counselors? It made you uncomfortable but you couldn't put your finger on what was wrong.

In each of these cases, the problem is the view that the Lord's Supper is "only a memorial."

The ones who serve "communion" in such contexts think the only purpose of the Lord's Supper is to help us remember Jesus' death. They deny this meal is anything other than a spiritual memory prompt.

Is that really all our Lord Jesus meant communion to be—a simple exercise aimed at reminding us of His death for us?

Certainly it is that, but it's also much more. It is a sacrament, a visible sign of an invisible spiritual reality, and it is nothing to trifle with.

As we've seen above in the text of 1 Corinthians 11, God Himself has warned us that when we eat and drink this sacrament in an unworthy manner, we eat and drink judgment and condemnation to ourselves. This is more than a simple memory prompt.

Sometimes my wife, Mary Lee, and I have opportunity visit other churches. Twice we've visited churches where, following the sermon and with no warning and no reading of the words of institution and no fencing of the table, plates containing communion cups and crackers were passed to us.

Once, it was during the singing of a hymn, but the second time it was while someone was giving announcements. It was unbelievable how quickly it was over. If you blinked, you missed it.

If we had been unbelievers, we would have had no idea what was going on or what we should do.

This was what the celebration of the Lord's Supper had become in both these congregations: a ritual devoid of warning, Scripture, time to examine yourself, and meaning.

It had become just a superstitious ceremony. Why do I say "superstitious"?

Because partaking of the Lord's Supper has no meaning apart from the

Word of God and faith. It is not something that communicates grace to us in and of itself, but only when those eating and drinking do so as a conscious response of faith to the promise of God's Word.

But there's another superstitious error we must equally guard against and this is the error of thinking of the Lord's Supper as a means of grace without regard to the faith of the one partaking.

Let me tell another story.

Years ago I was ministering in a small town in rural Wisconsin where the largest church in the community was part of a denomination whose doctrine and practice of the sacraments led the members of the congregation to believe that participation in the sacraments saved them and their children without respect to their personal faith.

One day I heard a knock on the door of my office at the back of the church, and, opening the door, I found two girls around the age of twelve standing there. I asked if I could help them, and they said they were doing a homework assignment and would like to ask me some questions.

Their assignment was to go into the community and interview people with different jobs, and they'd chosen the Presbyterian pastor as their subject.

We had a pleasant conversation, but I particularly remember one point where the two young women began to speak to each other as if I weren't present. Specifically, they were talking about their own church and their current attendance at a short series of confirmation classes preparing them for what they called "first communion." At one point one of these young women said to the other, "My dad says, after the class is done and I've done communion, I never have to go back again." She meant, go back to church.

What sort of pastor tolerates the practice of children receiving first communion who know once it's over they never have to do it again? What sort of congregation teaches its children that, once they've had their first communion, it has done its magic on them and they're safe? Similarly, how could anyone eat and drink as an act of faith when they're expected to listen to announcements as they eat and drink?

The Lord's Supper is a sacrament, blessed by God to all those who partake with faith in the Son of God who gave His life up for us. Without that faith, the Lord's Supper avails nothing other than God's condemnation and judgment. Congregations that think of this holy meal as "only a memorial" and congregations that practice it in a superstitious way without making God's requirement of faith clear have this in common: they are robbing the souls in their fellowship of the wonderful blessings which God has promised will attend this meal.

### The Lord's Supper is for sinners.

Jesus said He didn't come for the righteous, but for sinners. This is one of the most encouraging words He ever spoke. Think of it: when God Almighty took on man's flesh, it was for the purpose of saving sinners. Real sinners.

Nowhere is this as comforting as when we approach the Lord's Table and hear the words "let a man examine himself." Finding ourselves desperately lacking a righteousness of our own, what are we to do?

Well of course, come. Eat the bread of our Lord's body and drink the wine of His blood. Taste and feel the love that bought our redemption. Here we have our sure salvation, and He gave Himself only for those in desperate need.

But what if we're fearful of His wrath and sure that we are not worthy of His precious blood?

Well, then especially we must come. Not because we're wrong, but because we're right. We're sure of our desperate need and we must obey Him and, in faith, come.

*But how can this be?* you ask. *After those severe warnings Scripture gives about the dangers of eating and drinking without examining ourselves, how can you exhort sinners to come after we examine ourselves and find that we are desperate sinners?*

I exhort sinners to come to Jesus, to eat His body and drink His blood, because He Himself has promised,

> I am the living bread that came down out of heaven; if anyone eats of this bread, he will live forever; and the bread also which I shall give for the life of the world is My flesh.

The Jews therefore began to argue with one another, saying, "How can this man give us His flesh to eat?"

Jesus therefore said to them, "Truly, truly, I say to you, unless you eat the flesh of the Son of Man and drink His blood, you have no life in yourselves. He who eats My flesh and drinks My blood has eternal life, and I will raise him up on the last day. For My flesh is true food, and My blood is true drink. He who eats My flesh and drinks My blood abides in Me, and I in him."[18]

The Lord's Supper has been given, not to wound, but to heal tender consciences that look to the Lamb of God. Yes, we have many sins and our consciences accuse us of being unworthy, but it's precisely such souls who are qualified to come. Looking to the cross, we are to claim Christ's body and blood as our own food and drink.

Again, we are to come and eat and drink of His body and blood. He Himself gives the command.

If it is wrong on the one hand to come to His Table with no pangs of conscience, refusing the ministry of the Word and Spirit which bring us to see and repent of our sin; it's equally wrong to refuse the call of our Lord and His Spirit to come and eat and drink at the Lord's Table because we see and mourn our sins. It is not piety, but pride to deny that the body and blood of our Lord are sufficient to properly clothe us in righteousness for eating at His own Table.

Knowing how frequently tender consciences abstain from eating and drinking at the Lord's Table, I've taken to using a section from an old Scottish *Book of Common Order* as part of my own fencing of the table. This is the part of that liturgy that gives me great joy when I read it to the congregation:

> And although you feel that you have not perfect faith, and do not serve God as you ought; yet if, by God's grace, you are heartily sorry for your sins and infirmities, and earnestly desire to withstand all unbelief, and to keep all His commandments, be assured that your remaining imper-

18. John 6:51–56.

fections do not prevent you from being received of God in mercy, and so made worthy partakers of this heavenly food.[19]

The Lord's Supper is not for the proudly righteous. It's for those who are weak. It's for those who feel keenly how small their faith is, who don't serve God as they ought, and who are deeply sorry for their sins and weaknesses. It's for those who desperately want, once and for all, to be done with their unbelief and to keep every one of their heavenly Father's commandments.

Then—precisely then—they are to be reassured that the sin that remains within them does not bar them from God receiving them out of His great mercy, making them "worthy partakers of this heavenly food."

And then this most wonderful statement of all in the Scottish *Book of Common Order*:

> For we come not to this supper as righteous in ourselves, but we come to seek our life in Christ, acknowledging that we lie in the midst of death. Let us, then, look upon this sacrament as a remedy for those who are sick, and consider that the worthiness our Lord requireth of us is, that we be truly sorry for our sins, and find our joy and salvation in Him. United with Him who is holy, even our Lord Jesus Christ, we are accepted of the Father, and invited to partake of these HOLY THINGS, WHICH ARE FOR HOLY PERSONS.[20]

19. Adapted from *A Book of Common Order*, "The Order of the Celebration of the Lord's Supper, or Holy Communion" (William Blackwood and Sons, 1874), 173–74.
20. Ibid., 174.

*In the same way the Spirit also helps our weakness; for we do not know how to pray as we should, but the Spirit Himself intercedes for us with groanings too deep for words.*

—*Romans 8:26*

# CHAPTER 6

# *Prayer*

**T**HE CHURCH IN JERUSALEM WAS DEVOTED TO the teaching of the apostles, fellowship, the breaking of bread, and prayer—the fourth and final devotion of the Church.

Older now, I've lived long enough to be able to recognize some major trends, and one of the most serious is the absence of prayer during worship. I'm not talking about liberal churches, but conservative congregations who would see themselves as committed to the Bible and to the Lordship of Jesus Christ. During the worship of otherwise biblical churches, prayer is neglected.

What leads me to this conclusion?

If you are handed a bulletin, look for lines in the order of worship designated "prayer," and watch the time use during worship. There are announcements and lots of singing. Some of the singing could, formally speaking, be considered prayer, but spoken prayer is minimal. Sometimes there will be a brief opening prayer asking for God's presence and another prayer in connection with the offering. Between half and three-quarters of the worship service will be given to the sermon, after which the service will end with another song and (sometimes) the Lord's Supper, followed by the benediction.

Check it out yourself. Next Lord's Day during worship, count the minutes in the worship service that are spoken prayer. Most churches have worship services between sixty and ninety minutes in length, and the vast majority will spend less than five minutes approaching the throne of grace.

No prayer at the beginning confessing to God our sins and need of His mercy. No prayer of adoration. No prayer for illumination before the reading of the sermon text and sermon. No prayer of repentance and commitment following the sermon. No pastoral prayer[1] taking to our heavenly Father the needs of the congregation, our rulers, the Church around the world . . .

In past centuries, the pastoral prayer was similar in length to the sermon.[2] For instance, Puritan Cotton Mather wrote in his diary concerning the first service of the Lord's Day, May 13, 1685, on which he was ordained to the pastorate of Second Church, Boston:

> I prayed about an Hour and a Quarter, and preached (on John 21:17) about an Hour and a three quarters . . .[3]

Placing such a high priority on prayer during worship wasn't the exception, but the rule.

We may be tempted to defend the absence of prayer in our worship by saying we pray a lot individually and privately. We may justify ourselves by saying we speak to God when we take a walk, when we wake at night and can't get back to sleep, when we're driving or riding the subway, when we garden, work out, fish or hunt, and cut the grass—that's when we pray. After all, didn't the Apostle Paul tell us to "pray without ceasing"?[4] Also, Jesus said we shouldn't pray publicly, but in our "closets"; didn't He say we should keep our prayers "secret"?[5]

---

1. Historically called the "long prayer."

2. See Charles E. Hambrick-Stowe, *The Practice of Piety: Puritan Devotional Disciplines in Seventeenth-Century New England* (University of North Carolina Press, 1982).

3. *Diary of Cotton Mather, 1681–1708* (Massachusetts Historical Society, 1911), 98.

4. 1 Thessalonians 5:17.

5. Matthew 6:6 (KJV).

Yet when Jesus cleansed the Temple, he spoke to the onlooking crowd, "Is it not written, 'My house shall be called a house of prayer for all the nations'?"[6]

God's people have always assembled to devote themselves to prayer:

- Immediately after Jesus' ascension, the disciples gathered for prayer—120 of them.[7]
- Before choosing Judas's replacement, the disciples prayed together for God's leading.[8]
- It was on the way to public prayer in the Temple that Peter and John healed the man born lame.[9]
- When Herod had thrown Peter in prison and the angel of the Lord came to him late at night and cast off his chains, Peter went to the house of Mary, "where many were gathered together and were praying."[10]
- When men were set apart for the work of church office, their ordination was preceded by fasting and prayer.[11]

Scripture contains many more examples, but the point is made that the prayer at the center of the common life of the people of God was a corporate act. Together the Church sat under the preaching of God's Word. Together they ate the Lord's Supper. Together they fellowshipped. Together they prayed.

So again, if they prayed together, why don't we?

### Blind to Our Need

It's my fear that we don't pray because those of us in the rich Western world don't need anything—or so we think. Speaking specifically of the church in North America, we bear a stark resemblance to the fat and complacent

---

6. Mark 11:17.
7. Acts 1:12ff.
8. Acts 1:24.
9. Acts 3:1ff.
10. Acts 12:12.
11. Acts 13:2; 14:23.

church of Laodicea our Lord Jesus rebuked in His Revelation to the Apostle John:

> Because you say, "I am rich, and have become wealthy, and have need
> of nothing," and you do not know that you are wretched and miserable and poor and blind and naked, I advise you to buy from Me gold
> refined by fire so that you may become rich, and white garments so
> that you may clothe yourself, and that the shame of your nakedness
> will not be revealed; and eye salve to anoint your eyes so that you may
> see. Those whom I love, I reprove and discipline; therefore be zealous
> and repent.[12]

We think we need nothing, but in reality we are wretched, miserable, poor, blind, and naked.

Our Master tells us to ask Him for gold refined by fire, white garments to clothe ourselves and cover our shameful nakedness, and eye salve to heal our eyes so we can see. Our Master commands us to repent, but thinking we need nothing, we are silent. Our heavenly Father has promised to provide for all our needs, but we don't pray. Think of it. The Creator of the universe is awaiting our pleadings, yet we present none.

Sure, we pray for the sick during worship. But my fear is we simply want it to be clear we are sensitive and have compassion for those in the congregation who are suffering. We also pray for God's protection over the people of the congregation who are on a retreat or short-term mission trip. We mention our missionaries, the shut-ins, and maybe the president, but not much else.

Such prayerlessness is unheard of in Scripture. It is also unheard of across the five centuries since the Reformers restored biblical faith to the Church after a long period of captivity to Rome. Protestant worship has always been deep into prayer.

Until now.

Why wouldn't we pray when Scripture is filled with promises to those who pray?

---

12. Revelation 3:17–19.

> The LORD is near to all who call upon Him,
> To all who call upon Him in truth.
> He will fulfill the desire of those who fear Him;
> He will also hear their cry and will save them.[13]

Our Lord commanded His followers to pray:

> Watch ye therefore, and pray always, that ye may be accounted worthy
> . . . to stand before the Son of man.[14]

What a precious promise our Lord makes concerning His presence in our corporate prayer:

> Where two or three are gathered together in my name, there am I in the midst of them.[15]

Could it be clearer than this?

When summarizing the duties our Lord assigns us in our corporate church life, the Apostle James speaks of prayer five times:

> Is anyone among you suffering? Then he must pray. Is anyone cheerful? He is to sing praises. Is anyone among you sick? Then he must call for the elders of the church and they are to pray over him, anointing him with oil in the name of the Lord; and the prayer offered in faith will restore the one who is sick, and the Lord will raise him up, and if he has committed sins, they will be forgiven him. Therefore, confess your sins to one another, and pray for one another so that you may be healed. The effective prayer of a righteous man can accomplish much.[16]

With the positive comes the negative, so after all the examples of those who have prayed, exhortations to prayer, and promises of God's faithfulness

---

13. Psalm 145:18–19.
14. Luke 21:36 (KJV).
15. Matthew 18:20 (KJV).
16. James 5:13–16.

in answering our prayers, we also find warnings that the absence of prayer is a sign of godlessness:

> They say to God, "Leave us alone!
>     We have no desire to know your ways.
> Who is the Almighty that we should serve Him?
>     What would we gain by praying to Him?"[17]

We have an incomparable God. He is not one among many, but the only true God. He is the God who hears and answers prayer. So when the Church prays, she is not performing an act of religious piety which will earn credits toward eternal bliss. She is loving and declaring her trust and faith in her heavenly Father. She is glorifying Him and bringing her needs to Him, knowing He loves and cares for her.

Our Father knows our every need, often responding to us before we think to cry out to Him for help. The gods of the nations are blind, deaf, and dumb. Literally, they are not.

> Turn to me and be saved, all you ends of the earth;
> For I am God, and there is no other.[18]

### Pleasure and Prayer

Samuel Johnson once observed that "no man is a hypocrite in his pleasures." You might be wondering what on earth that has to do with devoting ourselves to prayer.

Well, let me ask: What does our worship indicate concerning our pleasures? Everything we do and don't do; all the ways we do what we do; every bit of it shows what gives us pleasure.

Also, what *doesn't* give us pleasure.

This book has pointed out that our congregations prefer preaching and preachers who speak calmly in a soft voice saying they might after all be wrong, and that we don't hire preachers who proclaim and address our

---

17. Job 21:14–15 (New International Version).
18. Isaiah 45:22.

consciences in the name of the holy God. Which is to say, we do not devote ourselves to the preaching of the apostles.

This book has pointed out that our congregations prefer to avoid true intimacy and one-another-ness. We don't enjoy having each other into our homes and eating together, nor do we seek to cross racial, ethnic, and socioeconomic boundaries to demonstrate the unity of the Body that the members of the apostolic church pursued and enjoyed at such great cost, particularly financial cost. Which is to say, we do not devote ourselves to fellowship.

This book has pointed out that our congregations prefer never having anyone barred from the sacraments, particularly the Lord's Table. We prefer not having the Lord's Supper mark the dividing line between those God has and those God has not called out, a function foundational to the biblical meaning and practice of sacraments. Instead, our pastors administer the Lord's Supper without warnings or fencing of the table, and our fathers commune their little ones without the permission of Christ's Church. Which is to say, we do not devote ourselves to the breaking of bread.

This book has pointed out that our congregations prefer singing and taking the offering and singing and giving announcements and singing and listening to the message and singing and doing communion and singing and receiving a blessing to . . .

Prayer.

We're convinced we are rich already and have need of nothing, so we ask our heavenly Father for nothing other than pro forma requests, particularly that He heal the sick and comfort the grieving.

No man is a hypocrite in his pleasures. Our church life makes our pleasures clear, and it makes clear which biblical devotions give us no pleasure.

We must reorder our hearts so that God's commands give us pleasure. That's the purpose of this book.

### The Work of the People

So how should we return to taking pleasure in prayer?

The main thing is to realize that we don't, and then to repent. Despite living in a day that hates any scrutiny of motives, the life of a Christian is a life devoted to the hard work of discernment, and that discernment should always start with ourselves and our own congregation. Remember the statement of the Apostle Peter that judgment should begin with the household of God?[19]

Next, a plan is needed, and let me suggest that plan begin with taking a look at the past worship services of God's people. We speak of this area of church worship using the word "liturgy," a word from Ancient Greek simply meaning "the work of the people." A worship service is worship "work" done by God's "people" assembled together.

Now, a word of caution.

Lots of people who would prefer the highbrow worship of St. Paul's in London to the humble worship of Spurgeon's Metropolitan Tabernacle will perk up their ears when you say you want to learn about the past centuries of the Church's worship. They'll assure you that all you need is *their* liturgy. Often they'll have a special label for their particular liturgy: they will call it a liturgy of the ordinary means of grace, incarnational liturgy, covenant renewal liturgy, or, simply, "scriptural" liturgy—so scriptural, in fact, that a sermon's unfaithfulness to the Word doesn't matter—the truth is in the liturgy.

Don't believe them and don't listen to them. Don't buy their books and don't learn their secret handshakes. Their view of liturgy is magical and mystical. It is not biblically faithful. Their faith is in their liturgy rather than in the God they claim their liturgy uniquely and purely worships.

All the word "liturgy" means is "work of the people." What you need to know is that the Church has always seen worship as hard work which should be done right, which is to say, done biblically. The only question you have to ask is what were the parts of the work and what order did those parts come in before our worship got rid of prayer?

Similar to our own time, five centuries ago the Protestant Reformers were faced with the necessity of reforming worship. Let's go back and see what were the parts and order of their reforms implemented in their work of worship.

Calvin, Knox, and the Reformers associated with Geneva taught that

19. 1 Peter 4:17.

the central principle of worship is this: whatever the New Testament does not command is forbidden.

We can have endless arguments over small details concerning New Testament worship, but let's keep this simple and peaceable. There have been intense fights over specifics. At times, parts of the Church have reacted against top-down mandated practices. Good accounts of Puritans' struggles for freedom of conscience can be helpful in understanding our present context.[20]

That said, at the time of the Reformation there was great consistency in the order and wording of worship, whether in Strasburg, Geneva, London, or Scotland.[21] Pastors and elders would do well to go back and study it.

## The Reformers' Example

During the first generation of the Reformation (1530–1550), the basic elements of Protestant[22] worship as it was reformed were as follows:

*Scripture verses calling congregation to worship:*

> Our help is in the name of the LORD,
> Who made heaven and earth.[23]

---

20. Those who want a deeper understanding of more recent Protestant worship—particularly in North America, but also among non-conformists in other parts of the world—would benefit from two works by Horton Davies on the conflict between Anglicans and Puritans surrounding the Act of Uniformity and the Great Ejection: *The Worship of the English Puritans* (Soli Deo Gloria, 1997); *The Worship of the American Puritans* (Soli Deo Gloria, 1999).

21. It's difficult to find a copy, but the best source on the reform of worship by Calvin and the early Reformed church is William D. Maxwell, *The Liturgical Portions of the Genevan Service Book Used by John Knox While a Minister of the English Congregation of Marian Exiles at Geneva, 1556–1559* (Faith Press, 1931).

22. We leave for another time discussion of the break between the Genevan Reformers and Martin Luther over the main principle governing worship. Lutherans held that, in worship, whatever Scripture does not forbid is permitted, whereas Calvin and the Genevans adhered to what we call the Regulative Principle: whatever Scripture does not command is prohibited. For this and other reasons, Reformed and Lutheran worship have always been distinguished by Lutheran worship demonstrating greater continuity with medieval Roman Catholicism than Reformed Baptist and Presbyterian worship. This is most notable in the Lutheran doctrines of the sacraments, and particularly their (in our view) tendency to formalism and *ex opere operato* (see note on p. 42). It was not accidental that the division between Calvin and Luther centered on the biblical teaching concerning the sacrament of the Lord's Supper.

23. Psalm 124:8.

Come, let us worship and bow down,
Let us kneel before the LORD our Maker.
For He is our God,
And we are the people of His pasture and the sheep of
    His hand.[24]


*Prayer confessing our sins:*

Lord God, eternal and Almighty Father, we confess and acknowledge
without pretense before your Holy Majesty, that we are poor sinners,
conceived and born in iniquity and corruption; prone to do what is evil,
incapable of any good; and that in our depravity, we endlessly transgress
your holy commandments. And so, in your just judgment, we deserve
ruin and damnation. But Lord, we are displeased with ourselves for
having offended you, and we condemn ourselves and our vices with true
repentance, longing for your grace to relieve our distress.

May you, therefore, have mercy upon us, most gentle and merciful
God and Father, in the name of your Son, Jesus Christ our Lord. And
as you blot out our vices and blemishes, extend and increase the graces
of your Holy Spirit to us day by day, so that as we acknowledge our
unrighteousness with all our heart, we might feel the sorrow that gives
birth to true penitence, which as we mortify our sins may produce
fruits of righteousness and innocence pleasing to you, through Jesus
Christ our Lord.[25]


*Scripture verses promising forgiveness of sins:*

And you were dead in your trespasses and sins, in which you formerly
walked according to the course of this world, according to the prince
of the power of the air, of the spirit that is now working in the sons of
disobedience. Among them we too all formerly lived in the lusts of
our flesh, indulging the desires of the flesh and of the mind, and were

---

24. Psalm 95:6–7.

25. Jonathan Gibson, *Reformation Worship: Liturgies from the Past for the Present* (New Growth
Press, 2018), 308.

by nature children of wrath, even as the rest. But God, being rich in mercy, because of His great love with which He loved us, even when we were dead in our transgressions, made us alive together with Christ (by grace you have been saved), and raised us up with Him, and seated us with Him in the heavenly places in Christ Jesus, so that in the ages to come He might show the surpassing riches of His grace in kindness toward us in Christ Jesus.[26]

## Absolution:

Let each of you truly acknowledge himself to be a sinner, humbling himself before God, and believe that the heavenly Father wishes to be propitious to him in Jesus Christ.

To all those who so repent and seek Jesus Christ for their salvation, I declare that absolution of sins in the name of the Father, the Son, and the Holy Spirit. Amen.[27]

## Singing of Ten Commandments (here or at beginning of service prior to confession of sins)

*Singing of a Psalm or hymn*—The claim that the early Reformers only used the psalms in worship is false. Even in Geneva under Calvin's leadership, songs with the texts of the Ten Commandments, the Song of Simeon, and the Apostles' Creed were used in nearly every service. In the *Strasbourg Psalter* of 1537, many German hymns were printed for use in worship.[28]

## Prayer for Holy Spirit's illumination of Scripture and sermon:

Let us call upon our heavenly Father, the Father of all goodness and mercy, pleading with him to cast his merciful eye on us his poor servants, not imputing to us the many faults and offenses that we have commit-

---

26. Ephesians 2:1–7.
27. Gibson, *Reformation Worship*, 309.
28. See Hughes Oliphant Old, *Worship* (Westminster John Knox Press, 2002), 44–45.

ted, through which we have provoked his wrath against us. But as he sees us in the face of his Son Jesus Christ our Lord—as he has established him as Mediator between himself and us—let us pray to him—as all the fullness of wisdom and light is in him—that he would guide us by his Holy Spirit to true understanding of his holy teaching, make it bear in us every fruit of righteousness, to the glory and exaltation of his name and the instruction and edification of his church; and let us pray in the name and with the help of his beloved Son Jesus Christ, as we have learned from him, saying: "Our Father, who are in heaven," etc.[29]

*Scripture reading*—Sometimes a chapter from the Old Testament and a chapter from New Testament were read here or elsewhere in the service. Prior to the sermon, though, the text from which the sermon was preached was read.

*Sermon and closing prayer*—Often the sermon ended with a prayer by the preacher. Here is a representative prayer by John Calvin from the conclusion of a sermon he preached on 2 Samuel 6:12–19:

> Now let us prostrate ourselves before the majesty of our good God, in recognition of our faults, praying him that it may please him so to touch us to the quick as to make us groan continually, so that we will run for his help and obtain mercy. And yet may we also be touched with such repentance that we will take pains to strip ourselves of all our carnal affections and lusts, so we might be renewed to the obedience of him who created us, and work in total holiness and truth all our life. And may he not only bestow this grace upon us, but on all people and nations of the earth . . .[30]

*Marriages and baptisms (if any)*—Yes, marriages were often held in connection with Lord's Day worship.

---

29. Gibson, *Reformation Worship*, 310.
30. *Sermons on 2 Samuel*, trans. Douglas Kelly (Banner of Truth, 1992), 277–78.

*Offering*—Typically this offering was for the needs of the poor among the people. The support of the church and her pastors came otherwise, through the civil magistrates.

*Long prayer*—This prayer, now often called the "pastoral" or "congregational" prayer, ended with the Lord's Prayer.

*Apostles' Creed*—This statement of faith was either spoken by the pastor or sung by the congregation.

*Singing of a Psalm or hymn*

*Lord's Supper*—The almost-universal practice among those churches aligned with Geneva was either monthly or quarterly celebration of the Lord's Supper. The liturgy of the Lord's Supper was lengthy. It involved substantial table warnings and exhortations, followed by extensive prayers prior to the people coming to the front to commune around the table. Not surprisingly then, through their magistrates, the "people" objected to the weekly celebration of the Lord's Supper Calvin and his fellow Reformers desired.

*Blessing*—Often called the "benediction," here is the one used most commonly:

> The LORD bless you, and keep you;
> The LORD make His face shine on you,
> And be gracious to you;
> The LORD lift up His countenance on you,
> And give you peace.[31]

The Reformers invented nothing in their worship. Rather, they returned practices to what worship had been in the Early Church. They reformed

31. Numbers 6:24–26.

Roman Catholic worship by simplifying it, turning the focus of the work of God's people in corporate worship back from Rome's sacramentalism and idolatrous Mass to singing God's praises, prayer, reading and preaching His Word, and the administration of the *two* sacraments, baptism and the Lord's Supper. Calvin and the Genevan Reformers largely copied the third century *Missa Catechumenorum* (mass for the catechumens).[32]

We must reorient our congregation's worship to follow the pattern of the great host of witnesses who surround us right now. They were men and women devoted to prayer. Let us reform our worship to the end that it's obvious to those who worship with us that we too are devoted to prayer.

> "This is the covenant that I will make with them
> After those days, says the Lord:
> I will put My laws upon their heart,
> And on their mind I will write them,"

He then says,

> "And their sins and their lawless deeds
> I will remember no more."

Now where there is forgiveness of these things, there is no longer any offering for sin.

Therefore, brethren, since we have confidence to enter the holy place by the blood of Jesus, by a new and living way which He inaugurated for us through the veil, that is, His flesh, and since we have a great priest over the house of God, let us draw near with a sincere heart in full assurance of faith, having our hearts sprinkled clean from an evil conscience and our bodies washed with pure water.[33]

---

32. "It was not the intention of the Reformers to depart from the central tradition of Christendom and innovate according to mere whim or mood. Rather they counted themselves as the faithful trustees of Catholic [i.e., universal Church] tradition, and if they simplified the Roman worship of their day, they did so with the intention of removing all mediaeval and sacerdotal accretions in order to achieve the simplicity and purity of the primitive rites." Maxwell, *Liturgical Portions of the Genevan Service Book*, 34–35.

33. Hebrews 10:16–22.

*I also say to you that you are Peter, and upon this rock I will build My church; and the gates of Hades will not overpower it.*

*—Matthew 16:18*

# PART 3

THREATS FACED *by the* CHURCH

**WE'VE EXAMINED THE CHURCH'S FOUR DEVOTIONS** and looked at what it means to practice each of them biblically. We've examined certain threats to each of them—some ways we misuse them, denying their nature and purpose according to Scripture.

There are threats to the Church, though, that are systemic. They don't latch onto our practice of the Lord's Supper only, for instance, but wound the entire organism. No part of the Church's life and ministry is safe from them; no work of the Church is beyond their corruption.

The next section deals with three of those threats. The number is arbitrary. My hope is that thinking through these three will be suggestive of other threats, leaving us better prepared to defend Christ's Church, "the pillar and foundation of the truth."[1]

1. 1 Timothy 3:15 (NIV).

*The naive believes everything,*
*But the sensible man considers his steps.*

—*Proverbs 14:15*


*How much better it is to get wisdom than gold!*
*And to get understanding is to be chosen above silver.*

—*Proverbs 16:16*

CHAPTER 7

# *Naiveté*

**I** **F WE ARE GOING TO CONSIDER SYSTEMIC** threats to the Church, the first we must recognize and learn to oppose is the repudiation of the gift of discernment.

The Apostle Paul wrote to the church in Philippi,

> This is my prayer: that your love may abound more and more in knowledge and depth of insight, so that you may be able to discern what is best and may be pure and blameless for the day of Christ, filled with the fruit of righteousness that comes through Jesus Christ—to the glory and praise of God.[1]

When God's love abounds, God's people grow in knowledge, depth of insight, and discernment. Every church should desire such love *and* its fruit.

But do we?

Usually not.

---

1. Philippians 1:9–11 (NIV).

## The Unpopularity of Discernment

Discernment is a tough sell among Bible-believing Christians today. Some thirty years ago I realized the Church now opposes discernment.

It was at the general assembly of my denomination. Each year I had been joining a team of pastors and elders who went to the Presbyterian Church (USA)'s general assembly to witness to Scripture's doctrine of the image of God in man and doctrine of sexuality. Our denomination endorsed the slaughter of the unborn and was preparing to endorse fornication, adultery, sodomy, and every other form of sexual perversion, so each June about fifty of us would show up and plan our witness to the assembly.

Many on the team had never met, so we did community building the first few days. The third day the assembly would be called to order, and invariably newcomers on our team would begin to cry, and their grief would last a day or two. Why?

Their grief came from observing the deep wickedness of the pastors and elders of their denomination. They heard what their fellow church officers were saying and saw how they acted in committee meetings and during floor debates, and they were appalled. Particularly the women—they were inconsolable.

For several years I watched the repetition of this clash of innocent hearts of true believers with the Sanhedrin wickedness of the assembly and denominational leaders. Then one day I was standing at the back of the assembly listening, and it hit me: the people of God weren't prepared to oppose evil because they had no discernment. They were harmless as doves without being wise as serpents.[2]

And this lack of understanding was not innocent. Battle against the wolves was needed, but no one was prepared for battle because discernment was absent. Back in their congregations, the love of God had not borne the fruit of knowledge, depth of insight, and discernment.

Then something else hit me. These men and women had no discernment because their pastors had taught them to despise discernment. It wasn't simply that discernment had too low a place in their congregation's priorities. No, the entire ethos of evangelical congregations was anti-discernment.

2. See Matthew 10:16 (KJV).

Of course, you might think this diagnosis is particular to mainline churches and doesn't apply to most evangelical congregations. Well, yes and no. It is true that mainline churches have abandoned all pretense of fidelity to Scripture, and evangelical churches haven't. Evangelical churches have great pretenses about fidelity to Scripture, but they're just that. Pretenses. Lip service. The willful, cultivated blindness that you see in most evangelical churches may be covered in more spiritual- or biblical-sounding fig leaves than their mainline elder brothers, but the willfulness and blindness are much the same.

Churches in North America have worked to promote naiveté to the status of a spiritual gift. Scripture commands us, "in understanding be men,"[3] but we refuse. Instead, we say, "in understanding be simpletons." "Cultivate childishness." "Commend the men and women who have remained spiritually immature despite ten, twenty, and thirty years of Christian faith." "Honor those who are on a milk-only diet and refuse to eat meat."[4] Contrary to the explicit teaching of the book of Proverbs, the Church in our time says credulity is not sin, but a fruit of the Spirit.

And, if we are honest, we will admit that our repudiation of discernment has gained us a lot. Ignorance and avoidance of God's Word and truth have turned out to be very profitable for our religious enterprises.

My father recognized this thirty-five years ago and warned,

> The evangelical church is sick—so sick that people are crowding in to join us. We're a big flock, big enough to permit remarriage of divorced people (beyond the exception Jesus allowed), big enough to permit practicing homosexuals to pursue their lifestyle, big enough to tolerate almost anything pagans do. We're no longer narrow; it's the wide road of popular acceptance for us.
>
> "When the Son of Man cometh, shall He find faith on the earth?" (Luke 18:8). . . .
>
> These are confusing days in the United Sates. Maybe God is building $20 million church edifices and $30 million electronic church motels. Maybe conviction of sin and repentance aren't related to salvation any

---

3. 1 Corinthians 14:20 (KJV).
4. See Hebrews 5:11–14.

longer. Maybe people need the success and prosperity theme to bring them to Christ. Maybe not.

To be sure would be terrifying for any American Christian who gets beyond dollars and numbers to the spiritual condition of church and society.[5]

Terrifying indeed when we remember that Jesus said, "Enter through the narrow gate; for the gate is wide and the way is broad that leads to destruction, and there are many who enter through it. For the gate is small and the way is narrow that leads to life, and there are few who find it."[6]

Working to throw the door of the Church open as wide as possible, we have turned "discernment" into a dirty word. Christians speak sneeringly of "discernment ministries," eliciting the desired disdain.

But what does Scripture say?

> How long, O naive ones, will you love being simple-minded?
> And scoffers delight themselves in scoffing
> And fools hate knowledge?
>
> .  .  .  .  .  .  .  .  .  .
>
> For the waywardness of the naive will kill them,
> And the complacency of fools will destroy them.[7]

## Refusing to See

There's an old saying that no one's so blind as the man who refuses to see. Why do we oppose seeing?

There are a couple reasons.

First, we love our sins. Discernment would lead us to recognize them as sins and call us to forsake them. But since they are precious to us, we resist bringing them into the light of God's Word. With good reason Scripture exhorts us, "Awake, sleeper!"[8]

5. Joe Bayly, "Who Are We to Judge?" and "The Power of Negative Thinking," Out of My Mind, *Eternity* (November 1982, July/August 1984), reprinted in *Out of My Mind: The Best of Joe Bayly* (Zondervan, 1993), 185–86, 199–200.

6. Matthew 7:13–14.

7. Proverbs 1:22, 32. See also Proverbs 1:4; 7:7; 8:5; 9:4, 13, 16; 14:15, 18; 19:25; 21:11; 22:3; 27:12 . . .

8. Ephesians 5:14.

The Early Church father Augustine put it this way:

> But why does truth engender hatred? Why does your servant meet with
> hostility when he preaches the truth, although men love happiness,
> which is simply the enjoyment of truth? It can only be that man's love
> of truth is such that when he loves something which is not the truth, he
> pretends to himself that what he loves is the truth, and because he hates
> to be proved wrong, he will not allow himself to be convinced that he
> is deceiving himself. So he hates the real truth for the sake of what he
> takes to his heart in its place. Men love the truth when it bathes them
> in its light: they hate it when it proves them wrong.

Augustine then turned to God in prayer and his prayer should be ours:

> You are Truth, and you are everywhere present where all seek counsel
> of you. . . . The man who serves you best is the one who is less intent
> on hearing from you what he wills to hear than on shaping his will
> according to what he hears from you."[9]

Second, discernment doesn't stop with calling us to forsake our sin, it
goes on to call us to expose others' sin also. Think of the Apostle Paul, particularly remembering Athens where he ended his sermon by condemning
the "ignorance" of their idolatry and calling them to repent.[10]

We find it difficult to preach sin and repentance to others because we
live in a society that has kept only one law on the books—the law that we
must all get along with each other. The endless blather about diversity,
inclusivity, pluralism, and tolerance we are force-fed each day is our society's enforcement apparatus of this single law, and it is directly opposed to
God's distinctions, biblical discrimination, and the discernment necessary
to honor both.

Knowing that biblical discernment puts God's people on the cultural
hot seat, the Church repudiates discernment, choosing instead to go along
to get along. Still, our consciences aren't good about it and we work hard
to make the case that our repudiation of discernment is, in fact, a Christian

9. Augustine, *Confessions*, trans. R. S. Pine-Coffin (Penguin Classics, 1961), 229–30, 231.
10. Acts 17:30–31.

virtue. We talk about the one without sin casting the first stone. We say love always expects the best. We tell the man or woman bold enough to say something discerning that, before he opens his mouth, he should take the log out of his own eye. Smugly, we command them, "Judge not, lest ye be judged."

But have you ever noticed this?

Do not participate in the unfruitful deeds of darkness, but instead even expose them; for it is disgraceful even to speak of the things which are done by them in secret.[11]

God commands us to expose the wickedness of the world we live in.

The Hebrew midwives did it. Moses did it. Remember his defense of the Hebrew slave? Nathan did it. Remember his confrontation of King David? Isaiah did it. Jeremiah did it. Amos, Jonah, and Malachi did it. John the Baptist did it, and lost his head. Jesus did it and He was crucified. Deacon Stephen did it and was stoned. The Apostles Peter and Paul did it.

Will we join them? Will we pray for the resuscitation of discernment in the Church today?

In the apostolic church discernment was a highly treasured gift of the Holy Spirit. It was understood to be critical to the safety and purity of the Church. Hadn't Jesus warned us, "Beware of the false prophets, who come to you in sheep's clothing, but inwardly are ravenous wolves"?[12]

The Apostle John gave a similar warning:

Beloved, do not believe every spirit, but test the spirits to see whether they are from God, because many false prophets have gone out into the world.[13]

It's always been necessary to exhort the Church to learn to distinguish between truth and error. Sixteenth-century Puritan pastor Richard Baxter exhorted pastors to be zealous in their work of exercising discernment

11. Ephesians 5:11–12.
12. Matthew 7:15.
13. 1 John 4:1.

among their flock, adding that it must be done both publicly and privately. But he warned pastors that their sheep would oppose them in it because of how few pastors there are who do it:

> [The people say,] "You are so precise and you keep talking about sin, and duty, and make such a fuss about these things, while pastor so-and-so, who is as great a scholar as you and as good a preacher, will be merry and joke with us and leave us alone, and never trouble himself or us with this sort of talk. You can never be quiet and you make more commotion than needs to be made; you love to frighten men with talk of damnation, when sober, well-educated, peaceable pastors are quiet, and live with us like other men."
>
> They will give you leave to preach against their sins, and to talk as much as you will for godliness in the pulpit, if you will but let them alone afterwards, and be friendly and merry with them when you have done, and talk as they do, and live as they, and be indifferent with them in your conversation. For they take the pulpit to be but a stage; a place where preachers must show themselves, and play their parts; where you have liberty for an hour to say what you (desire); and what you say they regard not, if you show them not, by saying it personally to their faces, that you were in good earnest, and did indeed mean them.[14]

In Hebrews, those lacking discernment are condemned for their childishness, for intentionally keeping themselves on a milk-only diet, refusing to graduate to solids. In understanding, they weren't men, but children:

> For everyone who partakes only of milk is not accustomed to the word of righteousness, for he is an infant. But solid food is for the mature, who because of practice have their senses trained to discern good and evil.[15]

Much of the Church's present repudiation of discernment has been justified by men who set the gift of discernment up in false opposition to

---

14. Richard Baxter, *The Reformed Pastor* (Banner of Truth, 1974), 85. Some edits were made in the first paragraph of this quote in order to reflect modern usage.
15. Hebrews 5:13–14.

evangelism. They claim there's too little time and energy to learn and teach biblical sexuality, the scriptural doctrine of the Trinity, Adam's federal headship, and the New Testament administration of the Lord's Supper. Their cry is, "Souls are going to Hell! Enough with the nitpicking. Just stick with the Great Commission!"

Yet doctrine is not antithetical to evangelism. Doctrine—biblical doctrine—is evangelism's marrow. Evangelism is calling men to believe the truth of God.

To disparage doctrine is to disparage our Lord's Great Commission. He is the One who commanded us to make disciples of all men, "teaching them to obey everything I have commanded you."[16]

The Hebrew church was rebuked for repudiating doctrinal maturity: "Leaving the elementary teaching about the Christ, let us press on to maturity . . ."[17]

Yes, I realize it might strike some as wearisome studying the ways we have abandoned the patterns of scriptural worship and family life of the apostolic church recorded for us in Scripture.

Yet what does Scripture mean when it reveals to us that Jesus is sanctifying His Bride, the Church? How can she be sanctified without having her sins and errors diagnosed? What purpose does Scripture have if not to sanctify the Church?[18] Why then do we cultivate ignorance of Scripture's record of the Church's family life?

My goal isn't to make people feel justified walking out on their current church.

No, my desire is for us to love the Church—not judge and condemn her. If we want to see the Church grow, we must not cultivate ignorance of the Church's weakness. Rather, we must study it carefully so we can join in the work Jesus Himself is carrying out in making her holy. Wouldn't you love being one with Jesus in the task of sanctifying His precious Bride?

Think of how we would read the Bible if we dismissed all the criticisms of the Church and her practices as counterproductive to the Gospel and evangelism.

16. Matthew 28:19–20.
17. Hebrews 6:1.
18. John 17:17: "Sanctify them in the truth; Your word is truth."

Reform is always attacked for being divisive, but, actually, it's the path to greater unity.

Didn't our Lord Himself pray that we would be one as He and His heavenly Father are One?[19]

19. John 17:11.

*For prior to the coming of certain men from James, he used to eat with the Gentiles; but when they came, he began to withdraw and hold himself aloof, fearing the party of the circumcision. The rest of the Jews joined him in hypocrisy, with the result that even Barnabas was carried away by their hypocrisy.*

—Galatians 2:12–13

# CHAPTER 8

# *Hypocrisy*

**T**WENTY YEARS AGO I NEEDED A CAR. KNOW-
ing my need and wanting to help, a brother suggested I buy his
dad's car. He said his dad would give it to me for a good price and I
bit on it.

This car happened to be a top-of-the-line Lexus. I told myself that it was
used, I was getting it for a great price, and I could sell it in a few months
for a profit. "How quick come the reasons for approving what we like."

My father-in-law was a godly man who drove old cars despite being
the owner of a large and profitable religious publishing house. He gave all
his money away and I was so proud of him for it. One of his executives,
though, drove a Mercedes. It always struck me as incongruous that this
employee drove a Mercedes while the man he worked for drove an old
Buick. Both cars sat in the parking lot giving testimony to the character
of their owners.

One day, however, something got into Dad and he went out and bought
a Mercedes. None of us ever saw the car, but we heard about it and the story
is still told. After signing the papers and taking it home, Dad had second

thoughts. Some say his second thoughts were because of the car's lack of acceleration, but I know better. It was antithetical to Dad's character for him to drive a new Mercedes.

He may have told the family he returned the Mercedes because it didn't have enough acceleration, but I know the real reason was his tender conscience. Trust me. Nothing he ever did, wore, ate, lived in, or drove was extravagant. Now though, in a moment of weakness, he'd bought a brand-new Mercedes-Benz. What could he do but return it? And who knows how much money he lost in the process of that repentance?

Did I learn from Dad's example?

No. I quickly accepted my friend's offer, even driving several hours to pay for the car and pick it up.

After writing the check, my friend's dad explained all the car's features to me, including a five-CD changer in the glove compartment attached to a bunch of Bose speakers. When the deal was sealed and I had the title in my pocket, I turned on the radio and began the trip home to Bloomington.

What a sweet ride. The car didn't have a scratch. The engine purred powerfully. The seats were luxurious. You sank into the leather.

As I drove, it washed over me that I finally had a ride worthy of me. Yeah, I was only a pastor, but my ride told everyone I was at least a consequential pastor.

I turned the radio up and five minutes down the road Pink Floyd was singing "Comfortably Numb." I should have listened.

### Deceptive Words

So what does this have to do with the Church?

In the days of the prophet Jeremiah, God sent this message to the people He had called out to be His own. They were busy at their religious duties, gathering at the temple of the Lord for offerings and prayer, but Jehovah wanted none of it:

> Thus says the LORD of hosts, the God of Israel, . . . "Do not trust in deceptive words, saying, 'This is the temple of the LORD, the temple of the LORD, the temple of the LORD.' . . .

"Behold, you are trusting in deceptive words to no avail."[1]

Why the three-fold repetition of "the temple of the LORD"?

The people of God were cocksure in their religion. No question they were the right people worshiping the right God. Were they not the sons of Abraham and Isaac and Jacob whom God had called out to be His covenant people? Was not Moses their lawgiver? Had they not been brought up out of the land of Egypt by God's mighty right arm? Did not Jehovah help them remove the wicked Canaanites and inherit the Promised Land where they were able to settle in cities they had not built and harvest fruit from trees they had not planted? Was not David their great king and his son Solomon their great wise man who had led the construction of this great temple? Had God not revealed His Law to them alone—not to any other people?

Of course God loved them. Of course God welcomed their worship. They were the called-out ones God referred to as "My people." How could God ever not receive their worship? How could God ever turn His back on their temple and the prayers they recited there?

Yet here we have the plainspoken message of God to His people: "Enough with your 'temple of the Lord, temple of the Lord, temple of the Lord' talk. Your words are lies. Don't trust in them. Your prayers are deceptions. They won't work."

Why not?

Because their worship was hypocrisy. While God's people were vainly repetitious in their prayers, their families, cities, and nation were filled with every kind of filth and wickedness. Immediately following His rebuke of their "temple of the Lord" mantra, God says:

> "Will you steal, murder, and commit adultery, and swear falsely, and offer sacrifices to Baal and walk after other gods that you have not known, then come and stand before Me in this house, which is called by My name, and say, 'We are delivered!'—that you may do all these abominations? Has this house, which is called by My name, become a

1. Jeremiah 7:3–4, 8.

den of robbers in your sight? Behold, I, even I, have seen it," declares the LORD.[2]

God's people were robbing each other, shedding the blood of their own children,[3] using the holy name of God to make their lies more convincing, and giving their worship and service to demons. But then they were gathering in God's place of worship and reassuring themselves and one another that God was their defender and deliverer. It makes you tremble. How terribly brazen of them. Did they think God could not see?

Well, actually, He could and did: "Behold, I, even I, have seen it."

## Three Examples of Hypocrisy in Worship

Not wanting to admit that our God is a consuming fire, we might try to escape the fear of God (which the Old Testament prophets constantly warned God's people of) by saying to ourselves that this was the God of the Old Testament, but Jesus has come and He is love. Such evasion won't work, though, because God is the same yesterday, today, and forever. This means today He is holy and almighty, and today He refuses to overlook sin—particularly the sin of hypocrisy in the worship the Church claims to give Him.

Three examples from the New Testament make it clear that hypocrisy in worship is no less dangerous and meets with no less severe consequences in the New Covenant than in the Old.

First, remember Ananias and Sapphira? Immediately following Jesus' ascension into Heaven, God blessed the church in Jerusalem with this terrible judgment and warning:

A certain man named Ananias, with his wife Sapphira, sold a piece of property, and kept back some of the price for himself, with his wife's full knowledge, and bringing a portion of it, he laid it at the apostles' feet. But Peter said, "Ananias, why has Satan filled your heart to lie to the Holy Spirit and to keep back some of the price of the land? While

2. Jeremiah 7:9–11.
3. See Jeremiah 7:31; 19:5; 32:35.

it remained unsold, did it not remain your own? And after it was sold, was it not under your control? Why is it that you have conceived this deed in your heart? You have not lied to men, but to God." And as he heard these words, Ananias fell down and breathed his last; and great fear came upon all who heard of it.[4]

God's judgment of Ananias and Sapphira reminds us of the time King David went out in great joy to bring the Ark of the Covenant back to Jerusalem. It was a day of holy joy. We read,

> David and all the house of Israel were celebrating before the LORD with all kinds of instruments made of fir wood, and with lyres, harps, tambourines, castanets and cymbals.
>
> But when they came to the threshing floor of Nacon, Uzzah reached out toward the ark of God and took hold of it, for the oxen nearly upset it. And the anger of the LORD burned against Uzzah, and God struck him down there for his irreverence; and he died there by the ark of God.[5]

A friend of mine is fond of saying that nothing makes the pagans tremble more than Christ's Church at worship. I would agree, but we must add that the Church at worship should cause Christians to tremble also. The singing of Psalms, hymns, and spiritual songs, the observance of the sacraments of baptism and the Lord's Table, the prayers, the recitation of the confessions and creeds, and the reading and preaching of God's Word each Lord's Day morning are the most serious and consequential acts of our lives. There is more at stake here each Lord's Day than any other time of the week. We are acting in holy matters in the presence of Almighty God. In worship, we call on Him to direct His eyes and ears toward us, yet He is a jealous God. We are praying, singing, and listening to God the Father, Lord of the universe, and He will not tolerate insincerity and lies. He commands us to worship him "in sincerity and truth."[6]

4. Acts 5:1–5.
5. 2 Samuel 6:5–7.
6. Joshua 24:14; 1 Corinthians 5:8.

The Church at worship is a Church gripped by reverence and awe.

Christian faith issues no license to stop fearing God. True Christian faith leads us to fear God more deeply the older we grow in our faith and the more holy we become. There's an old saying that in the godly fear and love embrace. This should always be evident among God's called-out ones at worship.

The second example of God judging hypocrisy in New Testament worship is the church in Corinth. The sins the Apostle Paul rebuked them for included lawsuits against each other in secular courts, using spiritual gifts to show off their superiority, parading their wealth at the Lord's Table while brothers in Christ at the table with them went thirsty and hungry, and living out their pride in worship despite the notorious incest in their midst. The church in Corinth was busy at prayer, preaching, singing, and celebrating the Lord's Supper, with no thought that God would not be pleased by their worship. They refused to judge themselves, so God's anger broke out against them:

> Therefore whoever eats the bread or drinks the cup of the Lord in an unworthy manner, shall be guilty of the body and the blood of the Lord. But a man must examine himself, and in so doing he is to eat of the bread and drink of the cup. For he who eats and drinks, eats and drinks judgment to himself if he does not judge the body rightly. For this reason many among you are weak and sick, and a number sleep.[7]

The hypocrisy of the Corinthian church's worship was the reason some among them were weak and sick, and others were dead (the meaning of "sleep").

The third example of the danger of hypocrisy in New Testament worship is recorded in the letters to the seven churches at the beginning of the revelations given the Apostle John, where we read these words from Jesus to the church in Thyatira:

> I know your deeds, and your love and faith and service and perseverance, and that your deeds of late are greater than at first. But I have this

7. 1 Corinthians 11:27–30.

against you, that you tolerate the woman Jezebel, who calls herself a prophetess, and she teaches and leads My bond-servants astray so that they commit acts of immorality and eat things sacrificed to idols. I gave her time to repent, and she does not want to repent of her immorality. Behold, I will throw her on a bed of sickness, and those who commit adultery with her into great tribulation, unless they repent of her deeds. And I will kill her children with pestilence, and all the churches will know that I am He who searches the minds and hearts; and I will give to each one of you according to your deeds.[8]

### God's Warnings for *Us*

I've been quoting a lot of Scripture, but I have to because there is so little fear of God in the Church today. Read the book of Hebrews and note its sober warnings to the Church. It says that those who harden their hearts against the Lord Jesus are in a more dangerous and damnable position than the Sons of Israel under the Law who rebelled against Jehovah. For instance:

Anyone who has set aside the Law of Moses dies without mercy on the testimony of two or three witnesses. How much severer punishment do you think he will deserve who has trampled under foot the Son of God, and has regarded as unclean the blood of the covenant by which he was sanctified, and has insulted the Spirit of grace? For we know Him who said, "Vengeance is mine, I will repay." And again, "The Lord will judge His people." It is a terrifying thing to fall into the hands of the living God.[9]

The New Testament warns that the reason the anger of God and His judgment of His called-out ones in the Old Testament was recorded in Scripture was to warn His Church today:

Nor let us try the Lord, as some of them did, and were destroyed by the serpents. Nor grumble, as some of them did, and were destroyed

8. Revelation 2:19–23.
9. Hebrews 10:28–31.

by the destroyer. Now these things happened to them as an example, and they were written for our instruction, upon whom the ends of the ages have come.[10]

We are to guard against hypocrisy and lies and sensuality and bloodshed in the Church today, not pointing at other churches and denominations we think are worse than ours, but examining ourselves and our loved ones seated at the Lord's Table:

> These are the men who are hidden reefs in your love feasts when they feast with you without fear, caring for themselves; clouds without water, carried along by winds; autumn trees without fruit, doubly dead, uprooted; wild waves of the sea, casting up their own shame like foam; wandering stars, for whom the black darkness has been reserved forever.[11]

The Holy Spirit speaks twice in Scripture of "synagogues of Satan."[12] The synagogue was the normal place of worship for God's people in the time of Christ. Jesus read and preached Scripture in the synagogue, and the Book of Acts documents that it was the habit of the apostles to attend worship in each city's synagogue and start preaching the Gospel there. So what is a "synagogue of Satan"?

A "synagogue of Satan" is a house of worship of the people of God where God isn't worshiped by the people of God. A "synagogue of Satan" is under the Devil's control, so it is no synagogue at all.

I bring this up because we must recognize that, today no less than in New Testament times, there are many places God's people gather for worship that are under the Devil's dominion and are therefore properly called "churches of Satan." Of course, God's people no longer reassure ourselves by the mantra "temple of the Lord, temple of the Lord, temple of the Lord." We have different mantras or shibboleths we repeat now in order to claim that God is pleased with our worship and that everything

---

10. 1 Corinthians 10:9–11.
11. Jude 1:12–13.
12. Revelation 2:9; 3:9.

is peachy-keen with us, our relatives, and those who join us in worship Sunday mornings.

What are those mantras?

Well, they differ by geographical location, ethnicity, and denomination, but every church has them. In my own Reformed or Presbyterian group, there are several mantras we use to signal to each other that we belong to God's people and have God's approval. Let me list a few:

- "Sola Scriptura. Sola fide. Sola gratia. Solus Christus. Soli Deo gloria."
- "the Gospel"
- "Doctrines of Grace"
- "the grace of God"
- "grace"
- "God's providence"
- "the sovereignty of God"
- "Westminster Standards"
- "grace"
- "confessional"
- "connectional"
- "graceful"
- "Gospel-centered"
- "covenantal"
- "Gospel-*hyphen*-anything-we-do-that-needs-to-sound-spiritual" (Gospel-motivated, Gospel-saturated, Gospel-transformation, Gospel-oriented, Gospel-cooking, Gospel-cleaning, Gospel-preaching, Gospel-singing, Gospel-ministry, etc.)

Now, of course God's people weren't going around literally saying, "the temple of the Lord, the temple of the Lord, the temple of the Lord," any more than Reformed or Presbyterian Christians are running around saying "providence of God, providence of God, providence of God." People in my own group don't walk around saying "grace, grace, grace." They just never stop talking about it. Grace this and grace that and grace the other thing and grace then and grace now and grace always and grace high and grace low and grace before and grace after and God's grace to you and God's grace to me and God's grace to both of us.

There are groups that never stop talking about being "missional." There are groups that say they're "in the city, for the city" and quote the prophet Jeremiah: "seek the welfare of the city." There are groups that are all about "celebrating the Eucharist" and "living sacramentally."

One year after buying the Lexus, I stood in the pulpit and I explained how owning that car had changed my preaching. I said I hadn't been as willing to confront our love of money as before. I said my preaching hadn't been as bold as before. I said a pastor should never own a car like that because he loves his car more than he loves God. I confessed my sin and asked the congregation to forgive me.

Hypocrisy is a sin that can be confessed and repented of like every other sin. But if you think you have none and would never sink as low as Barnabas or the Apostle Peter, keep this in mind:

> Neither man nor angel can discern
> Hypocrisy, the only evil that walks
> Invisible, except to God alone.[13]

---

13. Milton, *Paradise Lost*, bk. 3, lines 682–84.

*For the time will come when they will not endure sound doctrine; but wanting to have their ears tickled, they will accumulate for themselves teachers in accordance to their own desires . . .*

*—2 Timothy 4:3*


*A time will come when instead of shepherds feeding the sheep, the church will have clowns entertaining the goats.*

*—Charles Spurgeon*

# CHAPTER 9

# Gathering Goats

**M**Y WIFE RAN INTO A FRIEND IN THE SUPER-
market whose husband works for what their leaders claim is the
world's largest Christian mission organization. Their conversation
turned to a number of churches this friend and her husband had attended
the past few years.

She had nice things to say about each church. Then she brought her
list to an end by cheerfully exclaiming, "...and saving people! That's what
church is all about, isn't it!"

Like so many missionaries we have known through the years, she and
her husband were not committed to building up the Church, but they saw
that as no limitation on their work of "saving souls." Their organization
baptizes no one. They do not administer the Lord's Supper or do any church
discipline, yet they claim to be the world's largest mission organization.

The necessary question is, what is their mission?

This drew my mind back almost thirty years to an observation my dad
made about evangelicals' single-minded focus on evangelism: "Evangelicals

only want to see people saved. After they're saved, they think the person might as well die and go to Heaven because it's all over."

Does God have any plan for us other than being evangelized and doing evangelism, and is the church extraneous to this work? What *is* the work that Jesus has given us to do on this earth?

### Man's Chief End

The Westminster Shorter Catechism,[1] one of the most widely used Bible curriculums in the Protestant church, begins with the question, "What is man's chief end?"

The student is taught to answer, "Man's chief end is to glorify God and enjoy Him forever."

Glorifying and enjoying God are bound up with being born again, but they don't end there. So no, getting people saved is not all the Church is about.

In Heaven at the great marriage feast of the Lamb, Christ's Bride will be clothed in good works. Through these "righteous acts" the Church makes herself beautiful:

> "Let us rejoice and be glad and give the glory to Him, for the marriage of the Lamb has come and His bride has made herself ready." It was given to her to clothe herself in fine linen, bright and clean; for the fine linen is the righteous acts of the saints.[2]

Certainly the work of evangelism is one of the good works God has prepared for His Bride, but there is so much more. In fact, much of the work Jesus has given the Church is so foundational to the Church's evangelism that when it is neglected there is no evangelism. The irony is the Church

---

1. There are a number of excellent resources to help fathers and mothers teach this curriculum to their children, including Thomas Watson's *A Body of Divinity* (Banner of Truth, 1957) and G. I. Williamson's *The Shorter Catechism for Study Classes* (Presbyterian & Reformed, 2003). Also, shortercatechism.com is quite helpful. Great Commission Publications has a collection of resources based on a simplification of the Shorter Catechism called *First Catechism*.

2. Revelation 19:7–8.

neglects this other work precisely because we think it harms our ability to do evangelism.

Let me illustrate.

A couple years ago our congregation had a great sadness when one of our leaders confessed several sins he'd committed thirty years earlier. Because these were awful sins, this brother was immediately removed from office and the elders prepared a public announcement and censure which one of the older elders was asked to read to the congregation during Sunday-morning worship.

We regularly have visitors. If we'd thought about it, I'm guessing we would have hoped no visitors would show up that Sunday. Yet, as God ordained it, one of our young mothers had been inviting her neighbor to church for several weeks, and looking across the room as the censure was given she was horrified to see this was the Sunday her friend had chosen to accept her invitation. There she was sitting with her children.

Our young mother could only imagine the worst. I'm sure you're sympathetic to her misery.

Following the worship service, I had no idea who the woman was making a beeline to greet me at the door of the sanctuary. She was the first one out and she was burning to say something to me: "I can't believe it! I was just saying to my husband that we needed a church where there are real sinners. I know you won't believe me, but I'm so excited we were here this morning!"

We attracted that woman and her family to our church, but not because we were doing what people would call "evangelism."

The work the Church did that day was discipline. Public church discipline. And our elders would have been lunatics if they'd decided to do it Sunday morning during worship because they thought it would be missional or evangelistic, or because visitors would find it welcoming.

No, they did it because it was the right thing to do. It was work God commanded, and they obeyed, trusting Him to use that work to build up His Church:

Those who continue in sin, rebuke in the presence of all, so that the rest also will be fearful of sinning. I solemnly charge you in the presence of

God and of Christ Jesus and of His chosen angels, to maintain these principles without bias, doing nothing in a spirit of partiality.[3]

We wouldn't describe the censures and deaths of Ananias and Sapphira as "seeker sensitive," would we? Yet the Book of Acts records that, after their bodies were carried out of the church, "all the more believers in the Lord, multitudes of men and women, were constantly added to their number."[4]

## Authority in Disciple Making

Jesus commanded His disciples to go and make disciples of all nations. He didn't command His disciples to go and save people. To go and help people get saved. To go and tell people God loves them and has a wonderful plan for their life. To go and smile winsomely at their neighbors so their neighbors might ask them why they are always smiling so winsomely, and they could respond, "Because I'm born again and you can be born again too, if you just ask Jesus into your heart!"

Please don't judge me harshly for putting it that way. I'm just doing my best to tease out the things we think, but would never say.

If the Church isn't simply meant to save people, what work has God given her? We see this in the commission given the apostles by Jesus as they took up church planting in Jerusalem and across the Roman Empire:

All authority has been given to Me in heaven and on earth. Go therefore and make disciples of all the nations, baptizing them in the name of the Father and the Son and the Holy Spirit, teaching them to observe all that I commanded you; and lo, I am with you always, even to the end of the age.[5]

First, that word "authority." It's the foundation of the entire commission. God the Father has given Jesus His Son all authority in heaven and on earth.

If there is one reason a book on the Church is needed today, it is to

3. 1 Timothy 5:20–21.
4. Acts 5:14.
5. Matthew 28:18–20.

remind us that all the work of the Church flows from God the Father's authority in Jesus Christ, the Head of the Church. Sometimes we speak of Jesus being the "Head" of the Church, but too often it's only to deny that the Church herself or her officers have authority over us. And once again we see this bane of North American existence today: rabid individualism and autonomy.

Also rebellion—always rebellion.

People have told me they're not going to submit to any elders because they will never submit to anyone but Jesus. They say this is why they don't belong to any particular church, and when they say this they are not the least bit embarrassed to admit it. To them it's a biblical principle, and, clinging to it tightly, they feel superior to all the other simple Christians who don't know what they know.

You can't really fault such men, though, when you watch and listen to the shepherds of the Church today. Everything we do and say is carefully calculated to deny that we have any authority. Children in our churches call pastors and elders by their first names and everyone thinks it's wonderful. We pastors don't want to be authorities to anyone. We don't proclaim anything. We make a principle of not proclaiming anything. The pastor slouches in his pulpit and tells the people he has no authority. Only the Bible has authority, so he tells the people it's not his job to convict anyone of anything—that's the Holy Spirit's job.

And being good Americans, that pastor's people get further inoculated against submission to authority. "Yeah," they respond, "he's not my boss. Jesus is! I don't need any preacher to tell me what's right or wrong. He just needs to give me what the text says and leave me to apply it myself."

It's a closed loop of abdication and rebellion. You could make a case that pastors who refuse to preach to their people's conscience are responsible for their people having no guilt to feel or sin to confess, but you could also make the case that the pastor is this way because his rebellious people demand it of him. It was a condition of the search committee that he scratch their ears by kowtowing to their rebellion. Isn't this what the Holy Spirit warned us of?

For the time will come when they will not endure sound doctrine; but

wanting to have their ears tickled, they will accumulate for themselves
teachers in accordance to their own desires.[6]

My mother didn't cook a bunch of food and put it on the counter for
us to pick and choose. She had a menu for us, and that menu was based
on what was best to help us grow and be healthy. She made it varied to the
end that we learned to eat and like things people outside our home would
give us when we were guests.

Sometimes my mother fed us food we didn't like because that was the
discipline we needed.

Don't we need this in the Church? Pastors can leave the application of
God's Word to the people? Pastors can make a principle of never preaching
to anyone's conscience because that's the Holy Spirit's work? Seriously?

I'd laugh if this pastoral dodge weren't so prevalent and so utterly de-
structive to the souls God has placed under our care.

Try to imagine Deacon Stephen preaching to the Jewish leaders while
holding the principle that he should not apply the Scriptures to his listeners
and their sins. Likely he would have avoided being martyred.

Try to imagine the Apostle Paul writing the letter to the church in
Corinth in such a way that it was left to the Holy Spirit working directly
in people's hearts to bring them to the knowledge of their pride, lawsuits,
incest, and drunkenness at the Lord's Table.

Søren Kierkegaard puts it this way:

Imagine a fortress, absolutely impregnable, provisioned for an eternity.

There comes a new commandant. He conceives that it might be a
good idea to build bridges over the moats—so as to be able to attack
the besiegers. Charming! He transforms the fortress into a countryseat,
and naturally the enemy takes it.

So it is with Christianity. They changed the method—and naturally
the world conquered.[7]

6. 2 Timothy 4:3.

7. Søren Kierkegaard, *Attack Upon "Christendom,"* trans. Walter Lowrie (Princeton University
Press, 1944; Beacon Press, 1956), 138. In Lowrie's English translation, the word "charming" is left in
the original French, "*Charmant!*"

Jesus promised the gates of Hell would not prevail against His Church. What a comfort this is in our day when money and numbers seem to be all we care about.

## Moneychangers in the Temple Today

Sadly, I'm afraid money and numbers are what we mean when we boast of our commitment to evangelism. What we're really saying is that we want to do whatever we can to add people without having to discipline, feed, rebuke, clothe, or love them.

This playing to numbers bears a strong resemblance to the shopkeeping that went on in the Temple which led Jesus to whip the merchants and send their tables and products flying.

Yet the Church today has reproduced the mercantilism of the Temple in the time of Jesus, as well as the mercantilism of medieval cathedrals under the corruption of Rome which brought about the Reformation when Luther attacked Tetzel's sale of indulgences.

We sell our sermons online for a price. The numbers still come in (by which we really mean that the money flows in because we often don't even know the names of the "numbers"), giving pastors good salaries and the people convenient parking and pleasant-tasting coffee. Wanting our religion as cheerful as possible, we focus on having friendly greeters, Krispy Kreme doughnuts, smoke on the platform, deep bass from subwoofers (or a Casavant Frères pipe organ); bright, safe, and cheerful nurseries; and easy-on-the-eyes women reading Scripture, praying, ushering, taking the offering, and serving communion.

I've worshiped in churches with each of those things, but you know what? None of them matter. The Church grew when Jesus threw out the moneychangers and when Luther threw out the indulgence sellers. I'm sure it would grow again today if we threw out all this shopkeeper marketing we think makes our churches grow.

Sure, it's good to greet visitors and offer them coffee or tea. It's great to invite them to your home fellowship group. And yes, we hope they didn't have too difficult a time finding parking, but the Church isn't about that.

Church is not about convenience. It's about God, sin, righteousness, and judgment.[8] Pastors aren't supposed to attract sheep by convincing them how hip the preacher's tastes are. Pastors are evangelists and shepherds, not connoisseurs. Pastors who are shepherds—not shopkeepers—will hear the flock responding to their preaching with cries of, "Sir, what must I do to be saved?"

Men don't come to church to find cool or to find themselves. They've found themselves already and don't like what they've found.

Men and women come to church to find God. The Church is the tool God uses to call out His chosen ones. Men and women come to church to be saved from this sinful world and their own dark hearts.

## Born of the Spirit

Nicodemus was a religious leader who came to Jesus at night under cover of darkness. He began the conversation by telling Jesus that he knew He was from God because of the miracles He was doing, and Jesus responded, "Truly, truly, I say to you, unless one is born again he cannot see the kingdom of God."

It was a confusing statement, so Nicodemus followed up by asking, "How can a man be born when he is old? He cannot enter a second time into his mother's womb and be born, can he?"

If you took Jesus literally, it did sound ridiculous. That's how Nicodemus took it: Am I supposed to go back and become a baby in the womb waiting to be delivered a second time?

Jesus explained, "Truly, truly, I say to you, unless one is born of water and the Spirit he cannot enter into the kingdom of God." Not born again from our mother's womb, but born of water and the Spirit. Then He added something very helpful to those of us who think church growth comes through good shopkeeping:

That which is born of the flesh is flesh, and that which is born of the Spirit is spirit.[9]

The thing about flesh is we think we can control it. When we do church

8. John 16:8.
9. John 3:1ff.

in the flesh, we do the things we think are proven to bring the numbers into our shop. We have a website with good graphic design on which we bend over backwards assuring people we don't care what they wear.

We may have lots of parking, great coffee, and pounding subwoofers or organ pipes. And although we'd never say it, our actions make clear that we regard these things as more attractive than our great and wonderful Savior.

If flesh giving birth to flesh is what we're after, we'll design church in a way that controls variables so people can get in touch with their spiritual side without being inconvenienced. Church will be the best of both worlds: convenient location, nice or trendy architecture, no single-use plastic stirrers next to our coffee, a well-lit nursery with cheerful attendants who promise to give your little one back to you safe and sound after worship, music that's angst-ridden but emotive, touchy-feely preaching, and weekly communion freely available to anyone who wants some—all this and Jesus too.

But what if our goal is for men to be born again by water and the Spirit? What if we want men and women to be called out from the world by the Spirit of God, then baptized into the Bride of Christ?

If so, parking and coffee are relegated. Flesh gives birth to flesh, but Spirit gives birth to spirit.

Jesus' words about flesh giving birth to flesh and Spirit giving birth to spirit left Nicodemus confused again, so Jesus returned to His original statement:

> "Do not be amazed that I said to you, 'You must be born again.' The wind blows where it wishes and you hear the sound of it, but do not know where it comes from and where it is going; so is everyone who is born of the Spirit."
>
> Nicodemus said to Him, "How can these things be?"
>
> Jesus answered and said to him, "Are you the teacher of Israel and do not understand these things?"[10]

The danger is clear. The Church should never be presided over by pastors intent on building a supermarket for spirituality.

It's not really complicated. When Jesus commissioned the apostles to

10. John 3:7–10.

go and make disciples, He didn't say anything about coffee, tea, websites, carbon footprints, sustainability, or social media. What He did say was that all authority had been given to Him in heaven and on earth.

You see, church can be for God's called-out ones, or it can be for people of the world. It's never for both. Try to split the difference and you'll do neither well. There's an old saying among farmers: a grazed woodlot is neither good woodlot nor good grazing. If you have your cows graze in a copse of trees, they don't eat well and the trees don't grow well.

So make up your mind. It's one or the other.

If we want easy numbers, we'll use flesh to give birth to flesh, and our search committees will hire pastors who know how to give people a little religion without alienating them.

Kierkegaard was disgusted with the church of his time and had this to say about the modern pastor:

> It is pretty much the same now with the modern clergyman: a nimble, adroit, lively man, who in pretty language, with the utmost ease, with graceful manners, etc., knows how to introduce a little Christianity, but as easily, as easily as possible. In the New Testament, Christianity is the profoundest wound that can be inflicted upon a man, calculated on the most dreadful scale to collide with everything—and now the clergyman has perfected himself in introducing Christianity in such a way that it signifies nothing, and when he is able to do this to perfection he is regarded as a paragon. But this is nauseating! Oh, if a barber has perfected himself in removing the beard so easily that one hardly notices it, that's well enough; but in relation to that which is precisely calculated to wound, to perfect oneself so as to introduce it in such a way that if possible it is not noticed at all—that is nauseating.[11]

We must not allow the church to be a store run by a shopkeeper whose wares on display for the customers are a certain sort of spirituality a certain niche of the religious marketplace finds attractive.

Flesh gives birth to flesh, but Spirit gives birth to spirit.

One or the other.

---

11. Kierkegaard, *Attack Upon "Christendom,"* 258.

*There should be no schism in the body; . . . the members should have the same care for one another.*

—*1 Corinthians 12:25*

**HEAVEN**
*on*
**EARTH**

**WE'RE NEARING THE END, BUT THERE'S SOMETHING** that needs to be hammered straight before we're done.

The Church is a gift—a precious gift from our heavenly Father—and we must fix that in our minds and hearts. Dear brother and sister, never take the Church for granted. Many millions of souls across history have lived without the fellowship, love, and corporate worship of the Church, and it was a terrible thing they suffered.

During World War II, the German church had abandoned the Lordship of Jesus Christ for Nazi nationalism, but Bonhoeffer remained faithful. During the war he was invited to come home and lead an underground pastoral training institute. From that experience he wrote a short book of meditations on the Church called *Life Together*. As I mentioned earlier, this is by far the best thing I've read on the Church. I've recommended it to many.

From the midst of persecution, oppression, and loneliness during the Third Reich, Bonhoeffer (who was eventually martyred by the Nazis) wrote,

> It is not simply to be taken for granted that the Christian has the privilege of living among other Christians. Jesus Christ lived in the midst of his enemies. At the end all his disciples deserted him. On the Cross he was utterly alone, surrounded by evildoers and mockers. . . .
>
> . . . It is by the grace of God that a congregation is permitted to gather visibly in this world to share God's Word and sacrament. Not all Christians receive this blessing. The imprisoned, the sick, the scattered lonely, the proclaimers of the Gospel in heathen lands stand alone. They know that visible fellowship is a blessing.[1]

If you and your family have the privilege of being enfolded within the people of God in a local church, thank the Lord for His kindness each day. Your church may have many defects and sins. If you stop to think about it, likely you and your family have more. While we continue in this vale of tears, most of us sin enough against the believers around us that our sins assist them in their growth in patience and grace.

It was not a perfect church filled with good Christian people the Apostle Peter wrote to, pleading, "Above all, keep fervent in your love for one another, because love covers a multitude of sins."[2] Sin, repentance, and forgiveness are the steady-state economy of the Church. There has never been a church lacking sins. Thus, to maintain purity and peace, every church needs the covering of love.

"Love covers a multitude of sins"—that's the note we must strike here at the end. Not a few sins, but a multitude. Many, many sins.

Not well-intentioned mistakes, but sins. Wrongs. Evils. Things we know we should not do, but go ahead and do anyway. Things we know we should do, but refuse to. Things we teach while knowing what we're saying is opposed to Scripture—yes, pastors do that. Things we teach that are only halfway what Scripture says—which maybe is even worse.

Think about the church of Corinth. Back in chapter 8 we noted the

1. Bonhoeffer, *Life Together*, 17, 18.
2. 1 Peter 4:8.

believers in Corinth were proud of their superiority to each other, intellectually. They were proud while a man in their midst was committing incest. They were trying to get a leg up on one another by showing off their spiritual gift of tongues. They were taking each other to court, asking pagan judges to settle their disputes.

Their congregation was filled with division, but they didn't blush to come together and break bread with one another, hypocritically acting as if they were united as the Body of Christ. The sin among them was so pervasive and unobstructed by conscience or the rebuke of their pastors and elders that there at the Lord's Supper some of them made a conspicuous display of their wealth by pigging out and getting drunk while others had nothing.

In a number of ways, the Corinthians demonstrated that they meant evil toward one another. Through his letters the Apostle Paul listed their sins and rebuked them. Their sins weren't even close to well-intentioned mistakes. Had I not read the tenderness and love shown by the Apostle Paul for the Corinthian church in his letters to them, I would have thought the church in Corinth should have written "Ichabod"[3] over its doors and shut down.

Before you cluck your tongue saying no church should ever be given up on and that's the reason you're still in your pro-abortion, pro-feminist, pro-gay church of Satan, remember there were churches much worse than the church of Corinth. There were religious congregations God condemned as "synagogues of Satan."[4] There were also explicitly Christian congregations so far departed from God and His Word that Jesus wrote to warn them He was about to snuff out their light and close them down. You can read these warnings in the letters to the seven churches found in the first three chapters of Revelation.

So yes, there are many churches which have forsaken God's Word and Gospel. Another book could be written about how to recognize such churches, but this book is written for those who love the true and catholic (united across the world and time) Church. This book is for those who love her so much they are committed to studying her biblical callings and setting about the hard work of sanctifying her. It's for those who have faith to pray

3. See 1 Samuel 4:21.
4. See chapter 8.

for her sanctification, knowing that, as the Bride of Christ is sanctified, they and their families will be sanctified also.

It is no sin to desire and study and seek the reform of the Bride of Christ. Jesus came to sanctify His Bride. It is to this end that He Himself calls and ordains her officers. Pastors, elders, and deacons who are complacent in the work of sanctifying Christ's Bride make it clear they neither fear God nor love His sheep. Even worse are those church officers who persecute men and women who seek the restoration of the right preaching of the Word of God, the right administration of the sacraments, and the right exercise of church discipline.

But again, there is a serious difference between the sanctification of the Church and the judgment and condemnation of the Church. Yes, we must study and know the difference between the true church and the false church, but having said that, we must also firmly fix it in our minds and hearts that the Church is a precious gift given us by God and she is to be the object of our love.

We are not to hate her. We are not to be indifferent to her. We are not to judge and condemn her.

Sadly, though, this is precisely what many of us specialize in. We have condemned our present and former churches for not allowing children to take communion, for playing drums or electric instruments in worship, for not having an evening service, for not having small groups, for the length of the pastor's sermon, for not being solicitous toward us or our wife, for having a cliquish youth group that ostracized our high-school daughter, for having a youth group at all, for having some children in public schools, for not having any children in public schools . . .

One of my relatives told me she wouldn't come back to our church until we had women serving communion. Others say they won't go to any church that sings anything other than Psalms—and they must be sung *a cappella*.

Take the pet peeve of each of us, claim for it the moral authority of all that is good and right and true, and that peeve becomes a monster by which we judge other Christians and cause schism in the Church.

This is evil, but many of us have been guilty of it.

Back when Mary Lee and I were first married, we moved to Madison, Wisconsin, and began to look for a church. Growing up, the two of us had only ever been a part of three churches—I had gone to Blue Church in Philadelphia, then College Church when we moved near Wheaton. Mary Lee had only known College Church, where we met.

So moving to Madison required us to pick a church. We knew nothing about any of them except that a relative of a woman we knew at College Church had a brother who was part of a Baptist church there. We visited that Baptist church, but it was apparent they had an altar call at the end of every worship service, and we didn't like that. So we began visiting other churches, but each one had things we didn't like. Baptist, charismatic, non-denominational, and Reformed churches—our doctrine wasn't fixed at the time, so I'm sure the range of churches we visited was quite broad. Still, nothing grabbed us, so we would come home from church each Sunday disappointed and complaining.

One good thing about newlyweds is everything is new. They've left their families and they're focused on cleaving to one another. Part of the cleaving Mary Lee and I worked on was reading books out loud together. One of those books was the aforementioned *Life Together* by Bonhoeffer.

In the midst of our church hopping week by week, I was reading *Life Together* one Sunday afternoon, alone, and what I read hit me like a sledgehammer—in a good way. Immediately I stopped and called to Mary Lee, asking her to come and listen to what Bonhoeffer was saying. Here is the text:

> God hates visionary dreaming; it makes the dreamer proud and pretentious. The man who fashions a visionary ideal of community demands that it be realized by God, by others, and by himself. He enters the community of Christians with his demands, sets up his own law, and judges the brethren and God Himself accordingly. He stands adamant, a living reproach to all others in the circle of brethren. He acts as if he is the creator of the Christian community, as if his dream binds men together. When things do not go his way, he calls the effort a failure. When his ideal picture is destroyed, he sees the community going to smash. So he becomes, first an accuser of his brethren, then an accuser of God, and finally the despairing accuser of himself.
>
> . . . We do not complain of what God does not give us; we rather thank God for what He does give us daily. And is not what has been

given us enough: brothers, who will go on living with us through sin and need under the blessing of His grace? Is the divine gift of Christian fellowship anything less than this, any day, even the most difficult and distressing day? Even when sin and misunderstanding burden the communal life, is not the sinning brother still a brother, with whom I, too, stand under the Word of Christ? Will not his sin be a constant occasion for me to give thanks that both of us may live in the forgiving love of God in Jesus Christ? Thus the very hour of disillusionment with my brother becomes incomparably salutary, because it so thoroughly teaches me that neither of us can ever live by our own words and deeds, but only by that one Word and Deed which really binds us together the forgiveness of sins in Jesus Christ.[5]

The solution was simple. Mary Lee and I recognized our sin and repented. Really repented, joining, serving, and remaining committed to a group of believers called First Reformed Church of Madison throughout our years in Madison. It was a new church plant of the Reformed Church in America and if I were to describe it to you, you would not be surprised that a few years after we left the pastor of the church closed it down and it no longer exists. To us that church was beautiful, and it was as weak and needy and sinful as we were. First Reformed loved us despite how weak and needy and sinful we were, and we loved her back.

One happy memory from that church is the Sunday afternoon Bob Woodson, an elder who worked as a hematologist at the med school, showed up at our apartment door for a visit with another elder in tow. At the time we didn't have enough money for a phone, so Dr. Woodson had to come and visit us knowing he might well be driving a long way down to a run-down apartment off South Park Street for nothing. We might be gone, but on the chance we'd be home, he and his companion made the trip.

When we found them at our door, we welcomed them and invited them into our home, such as it was. Having no money, our furniture consisted of a mattress (no frame), a chest of drawers in our bedroom, and a stereo. But never mind: Dr. Woodson and his fellow elder came in and didn't complain about sitting cross-legged on the floor.

5. Bonhoeffer, *Life Together*, 27–28.

To this day I remember Bob's visit with delight. As the years have gone by, I've had occasion to thank him many times for loving his sheep when they were stinky and poor and had nothing to commend themselves to any church plant. Dr. Woodson did the work of a shepherd and loved his sheep. As the years went by, Bob had us into his home and we got to know his wife, Anne, and their little toddlers. We also got to know others in the church who accepted us unconditionally, and who soon allowed us to care for their children in the youth group and lead one of their small groups. Despite my pierced ear and Mary Lee's pierced nose—a big deal in 1976—they even allowed me to serve as their church custodian.

Was it a perfect church?

No, Mary Lee and I were in it.

Was it an orthodox Reformed church, doctrinally?

No, not by a long shot.

Were any elders women?

Of course. What do you think a Reformed church plant in Madison did to make themselves presentable to students and faculty from the University of Wisconsin?

Were gays and lesbians helped by the church's officers, or did they have a don't ask, don't tell policy?

Well again, this was Madison and it was a Reformed church plant determined to get everything right which stupid and intolerant evangelicals got wrong. Lots of InterVarsity leaders went there.

We loved that church and her people, and love covered a multitude of our sins, and theirs.

Now that I have your attention, let me repeat once more the truth we must end with: schism is a sin. Run from it!

At the head of this final chapter, we read the Apostle Paul's demand that there be no schism in the Church. He gives a similar warning to the young pastor Titus:

Reject a divisive man after the first and second admonition, knowing that such a person is warped and sinning, being self-condemned.[6]

6. Titus 3:10–11 (New King James Version).

"Divisive man" is the English phrase used to translate the Greek phrase *hairetikon anthrōpon*. It has been translated a number of ways, including "heretic," "factious man," "person who stirs up division," "divisive man," "sectarian," and "schismatic." Here in Titus 3 is the only occurrence of the Greek word *hairetikos*, from which we get our English word "heresy."

The original meaning of the Greek is something like "self-choosing," but it has a decidedly negative connotation. We know the self-choosing being referred to is sin because such a man is to be warned once, then a second time, then excommunicated.

It's no accident or mistake that in English "schism" and "heresy" are joined at the hip. "Schism" is a synonym of "division" or the more negative term "faction," whereas "heresy" usually refers to false doctrine. We see then that the connection between schism and heresy is that they both point to sins against the Church's unity and peace.

Truthfully, it was the certain danger of men being led into judging their church that kept this book from being published for so very long. Ten years, actually. I couldn't figure out how to explain what the Church should be and do without enticing men to condemn their pastor and elders. Intent really doesn't matter, does it? If the result of writing what should be is that men turn their backs on what is, more harm than good is done, and that's tragic.

So no. I am not calling you to leave your church. I am not calling you to sit in judgment on your pastor and elders, nor do I give you an exact formula for when to stay and when to leave your local church body.[7]

What I can do is tell you that wherever you find yourself (whether in a healthy church, a church in need of reform, or a church in name only) your first instinct should not be to separate or to judge God's people.

Your first instinct should be humility. Your first instinct should be gratefulness. Your first instinct should be love. Remember what the Apostle Paul wrote about love in 1 Corinthians 13?

The Church is our Father God's gift to His people. If you approach it as, at best, a necessary burden, you won't begin to glorify God as He intends

---

7. See the appendix for helpful material on the matter.

through His Bride. Learn to love the Church. Remember the good things God has done for you through her.

Imagine life without her.

Without her, Mary Lee and I would have been married at the county courthouse out in Salem, Oregon, rather than Mom and Dad Taylor's living room across the country in Wheaton.

What does that have to do with the Church loving me?

Mary Lee and I had committed the sin of fornication. We were Joe Bayly's son and Ken Taylor's daughter, and when we found out Mary Lee was pregnant we went down to the courthouse in Salem (where Mary Lee was living at the time with her sister, Janet) and applied for a marriage license.

Then we went and called our parents to tell them of the little child in Mary Lee's womb, and that we were getting married in a week or two. We confessed our sin to them. They heard us declare the sinfulness of our actions, they forgave us, and they said they wanted to know what day we would be married because they were coming out to be there with us.

Honestly, Mary Lee and I were floored! We thought when two Christian leaders' children have a wedding where the bride is pregnant, the farther away, the better for all involved. And certainly not in Wheaton where the gossip would be vicious.

Nevertheless, they were firm. They would be coming out. Of course, Mary Lee and I saw the stupidity in flying all of them out when the two of us could just go home, and go home we did for a wedding a couple weeks later. In Wheaton.

When we got back to Wheaton, Mary Lee and I were assuming we would be married in a private and quiet ceremony at our church home, College Church in Wheaton. Mary Lee's brother and his wife had us over for dinner, and hearing our plans they lovingly explained to us that it wouldn't be right to have the wedding in the church given Mary Lee's condition and our sin.[8] They weren't mean about it, and we didn't get angry. Again, we

8. This is not to say that fornicators should not be married in a church. I've officiated at wedding ceremonies in which the bride was pregnant, but it was always with the admission during the service of the sin and God's forgiveness. At the time of our wedding, though, it was clear the home wedding was a better option, being more humble and meek. Situations vary.

changed our plans and asked Mom and Dad Taylor if we could have the wedding in their living room.

It was a humble affair. The theme was repentance. Many tears and much joy.

Many there were Christian leaders of some sort, and no one condemned us. It was the Church and she loved us. Real good.

We had a multitude of sins to be covered with love and the Bride of Christ did it real good.

We moved from the front living room to the back family room for the reception and I remember there wasn't a dry eye in the receiving line. Only one couple's words stuck with me afterward. It was Ray and Beth Knighton. They hugged us, then warned, "Don't let the sun go down on your wrath. Don't ever go to bed angry. And if you have a problem and need help, just call us!"

Through the years, Mary Lee and I, then our children, and now our grandchildren, have received an endless stream of forgiveness, kindness, and love from the Church.

There was Charles Schauffele who got up each Tuesday morning and made coffee and breakfast for those of us who came to the men's prayer group at First Presbyterian Church in South Hamilton, Massachusetts.

There were Jack and Jean Fuller at First Presbyterian Church in Boulder, Colorado, who forgave me for reaming out Dr. Fuller in front of my Sunday school class.

There were my elder Don Jerred and his wife Evelyn, who waited patiently for Mary Lee and me to finish our fight in the car just outside their front door. We had called asking if we could come over and get help with our marriage. We arrived fighting, and patiently they watched and prayed.

As I write, such accounts of the beauty of Christ's Bride flood my mind and heart. Did I mention Mark Kraner, who showed up our first night in our new house in Bloomington, Indiana, saw we had no furniture, and immediately went out and bought us some? We'd never met him.

Did I mention Chuck Dykstra defending me against another elder's attack one session meeting when I couldn't defend myself? He was the barber. He stood 6'4" or so and was the best skeet shooter, hunter, and fisherman in the county. Here's what he read:

For the time will come when they will not endure sound doctrine; but wanting to have their ears tickled, they will accumulate for themselves teachers in accordance to their own desires, and will turn away their ears from the truth and will turn aside to myths. But you, be sober in all things, endure hardship, do the work of an evangelist, fulfill your ministry.[9]

Yup, the whole passage. She (the other elder) had been listing all the bad things about our church's financial condition. She'd come to the session meeting loaded for bear with five pages of figures, all in red. After half an hour or so recounting a financial tale of woe and pending doom, she looked at me and asked, "How much longer do you think we can stay in business if you keep preaching the way you are?"

There was a long, long silence.

No one said anything, but then Chuck cleared his throat: "I have a passage here I'd like to read."

This is the love of the Church.

For my woman elder.

For me.

For the entire flock.

Yes, I'm sure the things I've just written have caused lots of questions in your mind you're wishing you could ask me. Do I think it was right to enter the ministry if I had committed fornication before marriage? Why did the parents of the high-school students allow sinners like Mary Lee and me—with pierced noses and ears and all—to lead their youth group? Why did we go to a church with women elders? Why did I ream out Jack Fuller publicly? Did the senior pastor Bob Oerter know about it, and did he discipline me for it? Why did I agree to serve in a denomination that had women elders? Have I stopped sinning, or do the brothers and sisters in my congregation now have to cover my sins with love as these past congregations did?

The Church has never been clean. Jesus owns her, and He is the One who says He came for sinners.

9. 2 Timothy 4:3–5.

If you have the eyes of faith to see, you will notice how the precious sheep Jesus has chosen for Himself give constant evidence of needing His washing and love.

Let me close by returning to that tender rebuke our blessed Savior gave Peter after he denied his Master in Pilate's courtyard. You remember Peter was pestered by a couple young slave girls who said he was one of Jesus' men? Each time Peter denied it—the final time with curses.[10] Only a few hours earlier Jesus had warned Peter he would betray Him.

Then, after His resurrection, Jesus found Peter out with the men fishing, and over a fire on the beach Jesus cooked them breakfast. After the meal, Jesus called to Peter,

"Simon, son of John, do you love Me more than these?"

He said to Him, "Yes, Lord; You know that I love You."

He said to him, "Tend My lambs."

He said to him again a second time, "Simon, son of John, do you love Me?"

He said to Him, "Yes, Lord; You know that I love You."

He said to him, "Shepherd My sheep."

He said to him the third time, "Simon, son of John, do you love Me?"

Peter was grieved because He said to him the third time, "Do you love Me?" And he said to Him, "Lord, You know all things; You know that I love You."

Jesus said to him, "Tend My sheep."[11]

So now, I ask you, dear reader: *Do you love Jesus?*

10. See Matthew 26:69–75.
11. John 21:15–17.

# *Appendix*

**B**ACK IN 1996, I WAS SERVING A CONGREGATION with a history of schism, and I had taken the call knowing this history.

It was no surprise, then, that after four years a power bloc of the rich and powerful wrote a letter offering me good money to leave. It was an anguished decision, but my head elder and godly wife stiffened my spine and I turned the money down. This led to the bloc doubling down and, eventually, a number of us serving as officers of the church faced the decision whether to stay or leave.

At that time, I decided to read a very old (1673) copy of John Owen's book, *A Discourse Concerning Evangelical Love, Church-peace, & Unity: With the Occasions & Reasons of Present Differences and Divisions about Things Sacred and Religious.* Seeking an emotional catharsis, as I read this antiquarian volume I marked it up in its margins and underlined sentences and whole paragraphs.

In the end, the officers and I decided to leave. Knowing some would view our decision as schismatic, we issued an explanation which included the following text from Owen that I'd found to be the most helpful thing I read during that year of turmoil. I hope it's similarly helpful to those of you faced with similar decisions.

Note carefully how much Owen weights the decision towards staying and working hard for reform rather than escaping the pain and suffering that always attend reform.

◆　◆　◆

Wherefore when any Church, whereof a man is by *his own consent* antecedently a Member, doth fall in part or in whole from any of those Truths which it hath professed, or when it is overtaken with a neglect of Discipline, or irregularities in its administration, such a one is to consider, that he is placed in his present state by divine Providence, that he may orderly therein endeavor to put a stop unto such Defections, and to exercise his *charity*, Love and forbearance towards the persons of them whose Miscarriages at present he cannot Remedy.

In such cases there is a large and spacious Field, for *Wisdom*, *Patience*, *Love* and *prudent Zeal* to exercise themselves. And it is a most perverse imagination that *Separation* is the only cure for Church-disorders. All the Gifts and Graces of the Spirit, bestowed on Church-Members, to be exercised in their several stations at such a season, all *Instructions* given for their due improvement unto the good of the whole; the Nature, Rules and Laws of all Societies, declare that all other *Remedies* possible and lawful, are to be attempted, before a Church be finally deserted.

But these Rules are to be observed, provided always, that it be judged unlawful for *any Persons*, either for the sake of Peace, or Order, or Concord, or on any other consideration, to join actually in any thing that is *sinful*, or to profess any Opinion which is contrary to *Sound Doctrine*, or the form of wholesome words, which we are bound to hold fast on all Emergencies.

And farther, if we may suppose, as sure enough we may, that such a Church so corrupted shall *obstinately persist* in its Errors, Miscarriages, Neglects, and Mal-administrations; that it shall refuse to be warned or admonished, or being so by any means, shall willfully reject and despise all Instructions, that it will not bear with them that are yet found in it, whether Elders or Members, in peaceable Endeavors to reduce it unto the order of the Gospel, but shall rather hurt, persecute and seek their trouble for so doing, whereby their *Edification* comes continually to be obstructed, and their Souls to be hazarded through the loss of Truth and Peace; we no way doubt but that it is lawful for such persons to withdraw themselves from the Communion of such Churches, and that without any apprehension that they have absolutely *lost their Church-state*, or are totally rejected by Jesus Christ.

For the *means* appointed unto any end, are to be measured and regulated according unto their usefulness unto that end. And let men's present Apprehensions be what they will, it will one day appear, that the end of all Church-Order, Rule, Communion and Administrations, is not the *Grandeur* or secular Advantages of some few, not *outward Peace* and Quietness, unto whose preservation the *Civil Power* is ordained; but the Edification of the Souls of men in Faith, Love, and Gospel-Obedience. Where therefore these things are so disposed of and managed, as that they do not regularly further and promote that *End*, but rather obstruct it, if they will not be reduced unto their due Order and Tendency, they may be laid aside, and made use of in another way.

Much more may any refuse the communion of such Churches, if they *impose on them* their Corruptions, Errors, Failings and Mistakes, as the condition of their Communion: For hereby they directly make themselves *Lords* over the Faith and Worship of the Disciples of Christ, and are void of all Authority from him in what they so do or impose. And it is so far, that any men's *withdrawing of themselves* from the communion of such Churches, and entering into a way of Reformation for their own good, in obedience to the Laws of Christ, should infer in them a want of Love and Peaceableness, or a Spirit of Division, that to do otherwise, were to divide from Christ, and to cast out all true Christian Love, embracing a Cloud of slothful negligence and carelessness in the great concernments of the Glory of God, and their own Souls, in the room thereof.

We are neither the Authors nor the Guides of our own Love: He who implants and worketh it in us, hath given us Rules how it must be exercised, and that on all emergencies. It may work as regularly by sharp *cutting Rebukes*, as by the most silken and compliant expressions; by manifesting an aversation from all that is *evil*, as by embracing and approving of what is *good*.

In all things and cases it is to be directed by the Word: And when under the pretense of it we leave that Rule, and go off from any Duty which we owe immediately unto God, it is *Will*, *Pride*, and *Self-conceit* in us, and not Love. And among all the Exhortations that are given us in the Scripture unto Unity, and Concord, as the Fruits of Love, there is not *one* that we should agree or comply with any in their sins or evil practices. But as we are commanded in our selves to abstain from *all appearance of evil*, so are we forbidden a participation in the sins of other men, and all *fellowship with unfruitful works of darkness*.

Our Love towards such Churches is to work by Pity, Compassion, Prayer, Instructions, which are due means for their healing and recovery; not by *consent* unto them, or *communion* with them, whereby they may he hardened in the Error of their way, and our own Souls be subverted: For if we have not a due respect unto the Lord Christ, and his Authority, all that we have, or may pretend to have unto any Church, is of no value. Neither ought we to take into consideration any terms of Communion, whose foundation is not laid in a regard thereunto.[1]

1. John Owen, *A Discourse Concerning Evangelical Love, Church-peace, & Unity: With the Occasions & Reasons of Present Differences and Divisions about Things Sacred and Religious* (Dorman Newman, 1673), 77–81. A few spelling and paragraph changes were made, but all emphases are original.

# Recommended Reading

## For All

* *Life Together* by Dietrich Bonhoeffer
* *What Is an Evangelical?* by Martyn Lloyd-Jones
* *Authority* by Martyn Lloyd-Jones
* *The Mark of the Christian* by Francis Schaeffer
* *The Church Before the Watching World* by Francis Schaeffer
* The Westminster Confession of Faith

## For Church Officers and Their Wives

* *The Church of Christ* by James Bannerman
* *The Reformed Pastor* by Richard Baxter
* Book 4 (on the Church) of *Institutes of the Christian Religion* by John Calvin
* *Attack Upon Christendom* by Søren Kierkegaard
* *The Liturgical Portions of the Genevan Service Book Used by John Knox While a Minister of the English Congregation of Marian Exiles at Geneva, 1556–1559* by William Maxwell
* *Evangelicalism Divided* by Iain Murray

# Scripture Index

**THANK YOU**
to everyone who supports
**OUT OF OUR MINDS** through Patreon,
with special thanks to the following patrons:

**Cody Carnett**
**Jim & Annie Hogue**
**Matthew & Sarah Hoover**
**Matthieu LaCroix**
**Andreas Mack**
**Karl Russo**
**Adam Spaetti**
**Jeffrey Sparks**

To support the writing ministry of Tim Bayly,
including future projects like this one, go
to **patreon.com/outofourminds**

CPSIA information can be obtained
at www.ICGtesting.com
Printed in the USA
FSHW022138080719
59817FS